Into the Lion's Den

Into the Lion's Den

Steve Maltz

SP Publishing

Saffron Planet
PO Box 2215
Ilford IG1 9TR
UK
T: +44 (0) 208 551 1719
E: contact@saffronplanet.net

ISBN 978-0-9931910-7-7

Cover design by Phil Maltz

Contents

Preface
Introduction

Preface

Has the World really gone mad? And, if so, who am I to pass judgement? Perhaps I am just a trouble-maker, a deluded individual who wishes to draw others into my madness. Some may even call me a conspiracy buff, someone incapable of separating reality from fantasy and living on a shaky intersection of the two.

This is where it gets interesting and challenging. My researches have shown me that the first line of defence for those who are *actually* promoting and perpetuating this perceived 'madness' is to label their detractors *conspiracy buffs*. This is not a throwaway line, it is a purposeful deflector, an acknowledged tactic![1]

The second line of defence is a troubling one. This is where I am reminded that many who share my views are not the sort of people one would wish to be associated with, for example, the hard-line anti-Semites on the *far-right*. An effective tactic and one guaranteed to make you pause and perhaps reconsider. This is not even an 'enemy of my enemy is my friend' scenario, as there is no conceivable situation where I can be friends with the Ku Klux Klan, white nationalists and various shades of neo-Nazis. Yet the search for truth can take one across some hostile terrain. It's not all a cosy yellow brick road to enlightenment. In fact, it is *far from cosy*.

Let's work our way towards the kernel of our story. What we have is a failed global economic theory, redefined using techniques from other disciplines, producing a covert cultural infiltration, hidden in plain sight and resulting in an oppressive, totalitarian system that has made massive inroads into our modern Western society. So, there it is. You can see why it gets up the nose of the neo-Nazis. And you can also see how it can seem to be a far-fetched conspiracy theory, straight out of the pages of a Dan Brown or Frederick Forsyth novel.

But it's real, I tell you, *it's real*. It's no conspiracy theory. I just wish it were. And like all good plots it has an adversary, a nemesis, perhaps the only thing that can bring it down. And the name of this foe is ... Christianity, the variety that is exercised *according to the Maker's instructions*.

You really couldn't make this up. Let us now begin to fill in the finer detail ...

NOTES
[1] See Appendix A

Introduction

When the writer Martin Amis returned to the UK in 2006 after a two year stint abroad, he was asked what had shocked him most on his return. He replied, *"the most depressing thing was the sight of middle-class white demonstrators waddling round with placards saying 'We are all Hezbollah now'. Well make the most of being Hezbollah while you can. As its leader famously advised the West: 'We don't want anything from you. We just want to eliminate you'"*.[1]

This single episode perfectly illustrates the two greatest current threats to our culture in the West; the disruptors at our gates ... and the disruptors already within. Western society stands at the intersection of two forces, both fundamentally violently opposed to each other, but both working together, despite their differences, towards the same goal ... the destruction of the unsuspecting host, Western society. And what do they wish to see in its place? The former threat seeks the establishment of a fierce, oppressive and medieval kingdom guided by proclamations from religious courts. The latter threat can be summarised by a pop song, *Imagine*, written by John Lennon, where there is no heaven or hell, countries, religion or possessions and everyone lives in perfect brotherhood and love. A bit of a contrast!

The former threat requires no introduction, nor commentary. It is a well-known and broadly acknowledged threat and few social commentators would disagree. The latter threat is far more subtle and it is this threat that we will focus on in this book.

Before I do so, I wish us to think a little about a period of history many centuries ago in which we find a parallel to where we currently find ourselves in the West. It was a turning point in history, with the 'coup de grace' applied by an enemy invasion. The barbarians were no longer at the gates, but had poured through them, brutally imposing an alien culture on a people once known for refinement and sophistication. These people had been softened up through internal strife, class warfare and the over-reliance on 'immigrant labour'. They were also 'not currently speaking' to natural allies, who might have otherwise come to their aid. The army was depleted and lacking in focus. The taxation system was collapsing due to tax evasion schemes and the government was weak and corrupt, with many factions working against each other, to the detriment of society as a whole. The final factor was the fact that the 'barbarians' had already arrived, through mass immigration in recent years, a 'fifth column' lying in wait for a 'call to arms'.

These were the defining characteristics of the decline and fall of the Roman Empire in the 5th century AD. Could we be in a similar place today with the UK and Europe and other Western nations? How could it have come to this? Did no-one see it coming?

NOTES

[1] The Independent: 'Martin Amis: You ask the Questions'. 15th January 2007

Part One:
How did the World go mad?

Embracing
'the alternative'?

A couple of years ago, in *Hebraic Church*, I mentioned a startling discovery. It regarded a proclamation made by occultist Alice Bailey in 1948, a ten point plan to *wrench society away from its Christian roots*. Her plan involved the education system, the family, lifestyles, legislation, art, media, religion and the government. It foresaw the rise of interfaith initiatives, abortions-on-demand, easy divorces and the acceptance of homosexuality as a norm. It made uncomfortable reading mainly because her nefarious predictions have become reality in our current Western society and *no-one seemed to see it coming!*

But here's a thought. The average citizen may not have seen it coming, yet others not only saw it coming but were actively involved behind the scenes to bring this destructive plan to fulfilment. And what is most unsettling about this is that a plan conceived by an acknowledged follower of Satan seems to have been executed by a group of atheistic political theoreticians! Following the maxim of know thy enemy, in the first part of this book we will discover how this happened and grasp the implications for our daily lives.

Alice Bailey said, *"The Church must change its doctrine and accommodate the people by accepting these things and put them into its structures and systems."*

It's deeply troubling that we see that, not only has 'the Kingdom of the World' taken on, absorbed and internalised these principles as its new norm, but many of the 'guardians' of the Kingdom of God (the established and institutional churches) have also been enticed into their clutches.

And it becomes more frightening when we start to realise how this has crept up on us during the last seventy years. Because a group of atheistic political theoreticians had also come up with a plan about twenty years earlier than Alice Bailey. This plan has not been explicitly laid down for public consumption, but rather is a series of objectives that can be surmised out of the writings and utterances of the protagonists. The key points involved matters of race, sex education, rapid change, the undermining of authority, immigration, religion, alcohol consumption, law and order, the media, the welfare state and the family. A strange collection, but all part of a wider picture that will eventually become clearer.

Before we embark on finer details, there's another element that needs to be discussed, or at least introduced. First let me introduce you to a simple concept, that of *'roots and agendas'*. The premise is that we are all influenced by something else or someone else and this can be a matter of family background, peer group, intellectual leanings or whatever. We all have an *agenda*. It determines what media we consume (it used to be what newspaper we read, but this has broadened thanks to the internet), what political party we support, what causes get us riled and who we choose as friends. *No man is an island*, we are all connected somewhere. Our agenda may place us somewhere on the political spectrum or provide us with a faith in a higher being.

This agenda though doesn't spring out of nowhere, but rather there is generally a root that informs it, a cause that drives it. If you are a Christian, your family could be lifelong Methodists, Anglicans, Baptists or Catholics (or any one of hundreds of others) and, through your formative years you would have taken on board many of their teachings and customs. You could have a Muslim, Jewish or Hindu background and, as in my case, this could help direct your path, perhaps equipping you as a missionary to your own people. Then there is the matter of your lifestyle or personal philosophy before your conversion. You could have lived a hedonistic lifestyle of debauchery and self-fulfilment. You could have been a communist, a conservative, a green activist, a vegetarian, an animal liberationist, a feminist, a homosexual, even an atheist. You may have been a naturally spiritual person, or a rationalist, even a hardened sceptic. These are our roots. Even before God comes into our lives, we all still have a set of beliefs, even if it is just a self-belief.

So, to repeat, no man (or woman) is an island. It used to be easy, living in a connected world. We read the newspaper that aligned closest to one's political and social view and one trusted the BBC news, as delivered by radio and television set. The options on offer now, of course, are vastly more comprehensive and we add web channels into the mix, whether from official media organisations or from the growing band of independent free thinkers. And this leads me to a question that just a couple of months ago I would not have dreamt of asking.

What if you couldn't always trust your traditional news and opinion sources anymore? In fact, *what if – on certain issues - you should never have trusted them in the first place*? Is this safe old Auntie Beeb being disrespected? And what about that bastion 'of all that is right and true', "the Thunderer", *The Times*? Am I speaking treason now, because a part of me is starting to think so? But I really need to venture forth, because there's a real story here – one that the Mainstream Media (MSM) would not dare to tell, except as an oddity of a conspiracy theory from *someone perhaps a little unhinged.* You really need to stay with me on this one. As we dig deeper into our story you will see many examples that will confirm my position and the real beauty of the internet is that anyone has free access to all the sources that I will be quoting from, so that you can judge and discern for yourself whether it is me or the World that is going mad!

Although I still pick up news stories from the MSM, for opinion and commentary I now go elsewhere. My favoured grazing pastures are the extensive video archives known as *YouTube.* There I have been introduced to a whole subculture of 'alternative' voices, some 'discredited', marginalised and fallen ex-personalities from the prevailing culture, others home-grown products of the new age of independent 'no strings' publishing. In *Appendix B*, there's a partial roll-call of the indigenous species of YouTube cultural commentators, who I have drawn upon so far.

So I have defined a few parameters and set out my stall. Let battle commence … there's a story begging to be told.

Re-invention

2

We begin our story with a failed global economic theory. This is the fruit of the mind of the German Jew, Karl Marx, in the mid-19th century. His basic teaching, *Marxism*, was a critique of Western capitalism, seeing it as a struggle between the ruling classes, who own the means of production, and the working classes, who own nothing but their own bodies and who, for a standard wage, do the labour that enables the rich to get richer. In Marx's view, this system was unstable and would result in the working classes, as a result of a growth in self-realisation, rising up against their oppressors and creating a classless communist society, where everyone is 'equal'. They would do this through revolution, rather than evolution, so it was a philosophy of direct action and violent outcomes.

So, did theory ever become fact? Certainly not in his lifetime, though his theories were starting to stir things up in Germany and Russia by the time of his death in 1883. His greatest legacy though, is a bad one, with tens of millions of people dying as a result of various implementations of his theories, beginning with the Russian Revolution of 1917. Before we shift ahead to that time, there's another key player who needs to be introduced.

Martin Heidegger was a German philosopher, said to be, arguably, the foremost philosopher of the 20th century. This wasn't necessarily a good thing, just as Marx's 'greatness' wasn't either, but he certainly was very influential. His theories are far too complex to be fully understood by us mere mortals, but suffice to say, he was influential enough to be of great use to the Nazis. This made him a very dangerous person for humanity in general as he was providing the framework for a philosophy in order to tear down the certainties at the heart of Western culture.

There is a link between Marx and Heidegger, a third player who was to become one of the chief catalysts in our developing story. His name was *Herbert Marcuse*, a German Jewish Marxist, who was mentored for a short time in the late 1920s by Heidegger and attempted to devise a new philosophy that merged together these two great influences in his life. Remember this name, we will be finding out a lot more of this particular gentleman as we proceed. But, first, we return to the middle of the second decade of the 20th century, the start of the First World War.

The First World War was a great disappointment for communists and Marxists, as they fully expected the working classes to break the shackles of nationalism and refuse to fight for their country. They had grossly miscalculated, not anticipating the hold of patriotism for one's country above all and the 'rightness of their cause' as dictated by their Christian upbringing. For the Marxist theoreticians, the working classes had let themselves down and betrayed their class, the only success being the Bolsheviks in Russia, who followed the script, but consequently consigned their country to decades of totalitarian tyranny.

After the war, a group of these Marxist theoreticians in Germany began a re-evaluation of their philosophy, in the light of its failure to galvanise the working classes in Western Europe, who weren't revolting enough for their liking! *The Institute of Social Research* was founded, in Frankfurt Germany, in 1923. It was more commonly known as the *Frankfurt School*.

It is at this point that interpretive history forks into two, with two entirely different stories regarding the aims of this institution. There's the traditional, safe, view ... and there's the *other one*.

The safe view is supplied by the (supposedly) independent editors at Wikipedia. Here's how they introduce it:

"The Frankfurt School (Frankfurter Schule) is a school of social theory and critical philosophy associated with the Institute for Social Research, at Goethe University Frankfurt. Founded in the Weimar Republic (1918–33), during the European interwar period (1918–39), the Frankfurt School comprised intellectuals, academics, and political dissidents who were ill-fitted to the contemporary socio-economic systems (capitalist, fascist, communist) of that time. The Frankfurt theoreticians proposed that social theory was inadequate for explaining the turbulent factionalism and reactionary politics of capitalist societies in the 20th Century. Critical of capitalism and Marxism–Leninism as philosophically inflexible systems, the School's Critical Theory research indicated alternative paths to realising the social development of a nation."

This conjures up an image of a cosy inwardly-looking academic think-tank, funded, as we will discover later, as a vanity project by a politically-minded left-leaning philanthropist.

The 'other' view is loaded with dynamite because it places the Frankfurt School at the heart of a massive, covert conspiracy, churning out not just theory, but a plan – a long march – for implementation of its objectives, however long this may take, a plan that is finding fulfilment every day in our modern World.

The safe view would not warrant the thousands of words that I am devoting to this subject. It's the other view that is the source of the cries of 'conspiracy' mentioned earlier. This can be taken in two ways – one could either place the Frankfurt School at the heart of a conspiracy to bring down Western Civilisation as we know it or one could insist that the real conspiracy is to believe that the Frankfurt School is at the heart of a conspiracy to bring down Western Civilisation as we know it!

I am a subscriber to the first view as I believe that that is where the evidence leads. The main reason why many cannot bring themselves to agree with this view is that - as I said in the preface - it reads like a plot of a Dan Brown or Frederick Forsyth novel. I have to admit that the conclusions derived from the clear evidence seem to be *downright unbelievable*. But that doesn't make it untrue any more than the facts of Christ's resurrection are too unbelievable for us to believe in them.

So, here are the facts in summary form, which will then be unpacked. The eggheads at the Frankfurt School, by bringing in techniques from other disciplines, such as the psychoanalytical theories of Sigmund Freud, *re-invented Marxism*, taking it from the realms of economics (the battle of the classes) and into the very fabric of Western society, where the oppressors are not so much the ruling classes but rather the very institutions of Western culture. With the rise of Nazi Germany, they relocated to New York, centred on Columbia University and there was born the new discipline of *Cultural Marxism*.

And there it is, *Cultural Marxism*. Proof of the

divergence of views on this is demonstrated if you look at its entry in Wikipedia – there isn't one! Even 'fairies' has a Wikipedia entry and everyone knows they don't exist! Instead you are redirected to a section within the 'Frankfurt School' wiki page, labelled *Cultural Marxism Conspiracy Theory*. So Wikipedia editors have *nailed their colours to their mast* and, by doing so, have ironically exhibited a key trait of practitioners of Cultural Marxism, *censorship without discussion*. More of this later as we go deeper into our subject.

Continuing our overview, how on earth were these academics going to be able to introduce their views into society? Being centred at a pliable university campus, their initial strategy was through academia. To pull in the intellectuals they formulated *Critical Theory*, a simple system disguised as a complex one in order to hide its true intentions. Even its Wikipedia page admits that the article *may be too technical for most readers to understand*. In a nutshell it states that ideology is the principal obstacle to human liberation. In other words it is saying that our Judeo-Christian heritage and foundations are stopping us from being free! This all sounds very 'hippyish' and it may come as no surprise that the alternative culture of the 1960s was birthed by the minds of the Frankfurt School. I did warn you that we are going to venture into some very strange places. But, before we do, it is time to slow down and find out a bit more. Let's return to that period after the First World War when the Marxists were forced into their rethink.

Georg Lukács was one such man. In 1918, he became minister of culture in his native Hungary. He realised that if the family unit and sexual morals were eroded, society could be broken down. So he commenced a schools programme, which involved presenting graphic sexual images to children. This didn't go down well with the parents and he was booted out of Hungary the following year. Four years later he had a chance meeting with a wealthy Marxist Jew named Felix Weil, who put up the money for the founding of the Frankfurt School. Our story begins in 1930, when the school started formulating its controversial strategies under the leadership of its new director, Max Horkheimer.

Under this new leadership, the Frankfurt School was to move away from academic concerns to a wider remit, *critical social research*, which involved an integration of the social sciences, a significant development. Key academics brought in to follow this path were Eric Fromm, the psychoanalyst, Theodor Adorno, the sociologist and Herbert Marcuse, who we met a little earlier. Things were now going to get a little tasty. Fromm worked with Horkheimer on finding connections between the theories of Marx and Sigmund Freud. The area of attack here was social change and, in particular, the *role of the family in society*. These men were arrogantly going to interfere with a system that has worked perfectly well since God gave it to mankind as a gift. To further this, Adorno later became involved too, working towards a goal of the reinterpretation of the family unit. At all times, ideas were filtered through Marxist principles, using dialectical mediation, whatever that may be.

In 1935, when being a Jew and a communist were not exactly the best combination for thriving in Nazi Germany, the School was moved to Columbia University in New York. Two years later Horkheimer published the manifesto of the School: Traditional and Critical Theory. In 1941 Horkheimer moved to Los

Angeles, close to the film industry, later followed by Marcuse and Adorno. Five years later he returned to Germany, leaving the other two behind to continue their work in the USA.

It is curious to discover that every single main character in our story so far is Jewish (apart from the Nazi philosopher) and you can begin to understand those who see a conspiracy (Cultural Marxism) hidden within another conspiracy (a Jewish desire for World supremacy!) Yet a flick through the biographies reveals a diverse group of people from many different backgrounds, classes and countries of origin – there were no Facebook friends in those days! All were united, not by race but by a desire for change born out of a discontentment with what they saw as the evils of Western Society (and, to be honest, issues with their own fathers, for many of them!)

For laymen such as you and me, the best way to try and understand their approach and their motivations is to get some sort of handle on 'Critical Theory', the driving force behind all of their ideas. The simplest way of looking at Critical Theory is that it is a system where *everything is there to be criticised and deconstructed*. It doesn't offer solutions to the gaps left from what they may have destroyed, it is simply a wrecking ball bludgeoning its way through the certainties of Western Civilisation. One basic principle was to *reject the notion of objectivity in knowledge*. This is highly significant as it lays down the roots of the relativism that is one of the key drivers in the Western World today. In fact, the whole of *post-Modernism* – the predominant driver of Western society - flows from this one statement. It answers the question, *what is truth*? with the answer ... *whatever you want it to be*. They qualify this by suggesting that historical and social factors need to be taken into account, including a consideration of the situation itself and who is the one perceiving it. It leads to the situation of politicians and philosophers telling us what to believe. No room here for absolute truth! Although one could go a lot deeper into what is by its nature a dense philosophical system, it is sufficient for our understanding that we treat the millions of words written on this subject just as commentary, and to hold on to the single defining statement – *to reject the notion of objectivity in knowledge* – a rejection of absolute truth. Everything else flows from this.

Back to our story, we have Horkheimer scuttling back to Germany and we are left with Adorno and Marcuse to carry on the work in the USA. Let's focus a bit on Marcuse first, to see what made him tick, remembering how influenced he was by the German philosopher Martin Heidegger. Heidegger was down on many things, but with particular scorn directed towards technology, capitalism, materialism, religion and individualism. It was no wonder he thought little of the Western culture of the day. It was after reading Heidegger's book *Being and Time*, written in 1927 that Marcuse decided to become a philosopher. Both were concerned about the 'oppressive' and 'repressive' nature of the advanced industrial society in which they lived and Marcuse was looking for justification for his own ideas about liberation and radical action of the individual from this 'oppression'. Marcuse took from Heidegger what he needed and then discarded him, not just because of the Nazi connections but also taking a page from the timeless unwritten saga, *when philosophers fall out*. For Marcuse, the other didn't go far enough into the multiple forms that oppression takes in Western society. Marcuse was slowly becoming a rather radicalised individual, an activist as well as a theoretician.

Very soon he was to become a very active individual indeed ...

The True Teddy Boys

3

Here's a 1950s phenomenon, teddy boys. Although a purely English phenomenon, they were rebellious young men dressed in a style from fifty years earlier, the Edwardian era. They come to mind as they perhaps symbolise the first stirrings of discontent and rebellion against a world that seemed finally to be *getting its act together* in those post-War years.

In reality, they were pussy-cats compared to another couple of rebels, though in this case we are talking about fifty-something German Jews of indeterminate hair style and dress. These gentlemen were going to do more damage than a coach-load of teddy boys could ever dream of.

Herbert Marcuse and Theodor (Teddy?) Adorno were their names and we have already been introduced. Adorno kicked off the decade with a book, *the Authoritarian Personality*, a hugely influential book in the subsequent years. Sponsored by the *American Jewish Committee's* Department of Scientific Research, the book was a wolf in sheep's clothing. Ostensibly written to help quash the re-emergence of *Fascism*, it downplays the Marxism that inspired it, to make it palatable for those who believed in democracy. It introduced the *F-Scale* (F standing for pre-Fascist personality), as a way of determining authoritarian propensities, on the premise that Fascism is the worst kind of authoritarianism and it can be detected early in a child's development, with sexual repression a factor!

The Frankfurt School's dabbling with Freud can be seen here and Adorno reveals his true intentions by declaring that Fascism can result from religion and conventional middle-class values concerning family, sex and society. According to the book, budding fascists can be those who believe in obedience and respect for authority, or have negative views on homosexuality, or who have a high view of personal honour.

What is happening here? You can understand the fear people had that Fascism may rise again and who better to teach the American social scientists than a German Jewish academic? Remembering the goal of the Frankfurt School concerning the family and Christianity, we now have the germ of an idea, that those who are brought up to have a high view of both ... *possibly have fascist tendencies*! This idea is going to come back and haunt us all, as this story progresses.

Moving on to Herbert Marcuse, he agreed with Adorno that Fascism can be traced back to psychological and sexual repression but then he switched things round. He stated that the good guys, *the anti-fascists*, would be the opposite, people defined by psychological and sexual liberation! He introduced all this in his first influential book, *Eros and Civilisation*, published in 1955. Here he made proposals that were eventually to ignite an explosion in the following decade. He suggested that the prevailing technological, capitalist society traps people by limiting their sexual libido, turning sex into a commodity (thought that one had been around since the days of Rahab!) and using religion and morality to suppress these natural instincts, through its promotion of monogamy and aversion to sexual perversion.

Let it all hang out! proclaimed Marcuse. *A suppressed*

sexuality is for fascists! It should be no surprise when the permissive Sixties took on these ideas and an aged German Jewish philosopher became a sex guru for a generation, even coining the slogan *Make love not war!* So, what have we learned so far in this Chapter? That, *allegedly*, the propensity for Fascism is limited to those from a traditional Christian family background and that only rampant sexuality can thwart these impulses! Isn't it amazing how a German accent and a book full of indecipherable concepts can convince the gullible that right is wrong and wrong is right! Remember, the chief objective of Critical Theory was the denial of absolute truth. Adorno and Marcuse are playing around dangerously with the truth and the amazing thing is that not only were otherwise sensible people listening to them, but that these skewed ideas would gain traction in the subsequent years.

The 1950s were also known for another related event, led by another 'teddy boy', though one who 'batted for the other side'. His name was Senator Joseph McCarthy and his name has since entered the lexicon of infamy, through the phenomenon of *McCarthyism*. Wikipedia defines this as, *"the practice of making accusations of subversion or treason without proper regard for evidence"*. If such a negative term can be coined from the actions of an individual, then that individual was either a nasty bit of stuff, or he has been unfairly vilified.

Like many of you I have been brought up believing the very worst of Senator Joseph McCarthy. Has this been justified? Let's start with the facts. McCarthy was the man most associated with the 'witch-hunts' for secret communists in American public office and other influential places. His 'reign of terror' started in 1950 in a speech at the Republican Women's Club of Wheeling, West Virginia with his opening salvo, *"I have here in my hands a list of names"*. He had in his hand a list of 205 names of alleged secret members of the Communist Party who were working in the State Department of the US government. In a noisy, confrontational and controversial four years campaign he wasn't able to uncover a single communist. He died in 1957, supposedly (but never proven) as a result of alcoholism.

So while the Marxists Adorno and Marcuse and others from the Frankfurt School were sowing seeds of destruction for Western society 'in plain sight' of academia, public attention was instead focussed on those who were doing the same covertly, as spies for Soviet Russia in prominent positions in the American government. The whole thing, conducted in the full view of the media, was a mess, and served only to discredit the very real hunt for subversives, many of whom seem to have got away with it over a long period. Also, whereas the spies were acting in the short-term economic and political interest of communist Russia, the academic subversives were still playing the 'long game', drip-feeding Marxist ideas into Western culture.

One well-publicised recipient of McCarthy's attention was the film industry in Hollywood. Being at the heart of popular culture, these people had a firm grip on hearts and minds and so were successfully able, at the time, to paint themselves as innocent victims of a 'witch-hunt'. This was demonstrated by the popularity of the play *The Crucible* by Arthur Miller, performed as a stage play in 1953 and a film in 1957, then later re-released in 1996. Inspired by the Salem witchcraft trials in the 17th century, it was a thinly-veiled reaction to the anti-communist 'witch hunt' by McCarthy and the *House Un-American Activities Committee* (HUAC). Miller was fined and blacklisted for his 'associations', though this was overturned in 1958. The fact remains, though, that he was at the very least a communist sympathiser and had actually sent in an application to join the Communist Party in 1939 (though he later claimed that he thought he was signing up for a study course on Marxism).

Although Hollywood was a persistent target for the HUAC, very little real evidence surfaced. Yet we should judge people by their fruit and, although many may not have been out-and-out Communists, the subtle influence of Cultural Marxism was beginning to bite. This was reflected in the shifting emphasis in the films produced, away from those reinforcing the Judeo-Christian bedrock of stable family relationships and wholesome living and towards the situation we find ourselves in today, where even family films depict casual sex, adultery, criminality and a dubious moral base. The 'envelope' is continually being pushed, with barriers of good taste and cultural taboos being broken continuously, *as if this is a good thing and an end in its own right*. They call this 'progress' and we are going to see this term pop up again and again and used by those who feel they are part of a positive move of progression. They call themselves 'progressives' and one wonders *what actually they are progressing towards*, though it is clear what they are leaving behind. Where will this end? It is very troubling and we really need to fear for our children and grandchildren as to what kind of 'culture' they are going to inherit from us.

History, as we saw, was not kind to Joseph McCarthy and, until the 1990s, the standard party line was that although there was an active Communist Party in America in the 1950s, it was small and ineffectual, unfairly persecuted by McCarthy and his gang, which also included Edgar Hoover, the head of the FBI, and Richard Nixon, future president. All three have become cultural bogeymen, in fact, for different reasons. History may have to answer some difficult questions regarding this, though, as the *real* conspiracy unfolds.

When the Soviet Union collapsed in the late 1980s, some documents held in secret places in Moscow became available, including some pertinent to espionage efforts in the USA during the 1950s. One thing that was discovered was that the 'small and ineffectual' Communist Party in America was being subsidised by the Soviet Union at up to $3 million a year, up until the 1980s and was far more active than originally thought. It appears that McCarthy was correct all along and, if he had been less clumsy and heavy-handed in his efforts, perhaps one or two of the Soviet spies could have been wheedled out, including those who sold atomic secrets (mind you, the parity in atomic weaponry did actually ensure an era of relative peace, so a nuclear Russia may have been, ironically, a good thing!).

The other thing that was discovered in these archives was that the Americans had cracked the Soviet spy codes during the 1940s, in a secret project named Venona and had intercepted nearly 3000 messages sent from Russia to their spies throughout the USA. They even discerned code names for 'enemy' entities: Zionists were 'rats', San Francisco was 'Babylon' and Washington DC was 'Carthage'. It turned out that 350 Americans were Soviet spies during the war years, including 16 in the OSS, the agency later to become the

CIA. None of this information, though, was available to McCarthy at that time as not a single person accused as a Communist spy by his committee was actually mentioned in the Venona papers.

Nevertheless there was a lot of active spying going on at the time, so McCarthy was right in principle. The question that needs to be asked is why was McCarthy so vilified, even after the revelation of the Venona papers? It appears that some historians believe them to be forgeries, in order not to disrupt their particular view of history. They have no proof for this, just a desperate clinging to their ideological biases. Such is the hold that Marxism can have on its victims, this seems to be a spiritual bondage that doesn't leave without a fight! The biggest mystery in all of this, whether considering the modern day apologists, or those who were involved in Soviet espionage during the 1950s, is how they can condone a regime that not only failed but that caused the deaths of over 100 million, mostly of its own, people!

Rebellion! 4

There is much rose-tinted nostalgia regarding the 1960s, even among those now who were not even born then. If there was one man who did more to create the framework for the major shifts during that decade it was not John Lennon or Elvis Presley or Timothy Leary or Martin Luther King or John Kennedy or Bob Dylan, but it was our sixty-something German Jewish Marxist academic, *Herbert Marcuse himself*.

Critical Theory, the driving force of Cultural Marxism, is all about tearing down institutions that form the bedrock of our culture, with a particular strategy of re-defining the family. It is purely destructive and is very much tied in with the Marxist ideology of control of the collective and the squashing of the individual. It is '1984 personified', interesting as George Orwell was a socialist writing at a time when the Frankfurt School was beginning to make its sinister inroads. It is interesting that the 1960s birthed the *counter-culture* and we can now begin to grasp that this was not initiated by a bunch of idealistic hippies, but there were other forces at play here.

Herbert Marcuse, sex guru. Through the message of his increasingly read *Eros and Civilisation*, he was subtly declaring the hidden message, *prove you ain't a potential fascist, get laid!* Remember, his philosophy, shared with his co-patriot Theodor Adorno, identified Fascism with sexual morality, family values and a Christian lifestyle. How better can you cleanse yourself from any unsociable right-wing tendencies than to indulge your fleshy appetites! This was aided by the advent of the birth control pill at the beginning of the decade, so significant that it was referred to as just 'the Pill', the chemical gateway to guilt-free sex. And, in the case of the odd 'accident', convenient abortions were made legally available in the UK as the result of the 1967 Abortion Act. Interestingly, convenience abortions were made legal as early as 1919 in Soviet Russia.

Marcuse's influence on the 1960s was profound. For him, the traditions of the family and of a Christian lifestyle were repressive and worth overthrowing, as was any adherence to objective truth. Everything is up to the individual, breaking free of shackles, a philosophy worryingly but significantly similar to the Satanist creed of Aleister Crowley, *do what you wilt shall be the whole of the law* (a corruption of Matthew 22:36-40). The Children of the 1960s were free to romp around and indulge themselves, but still benefitted from the affluence provided for them by their hard-working parents, who had largely triumphed over the post-war austerity measures by providing their children with a safe, secure upbringing. And what was the payback? Rather than rebels without a cause, they were *rebels with big cars*.

But Marcuse had a lot more in his locker. He'd only just got started! In 1964 he wrote *One Dimensional Man*, described by Douglas Kellner as *one of the most subversive books of the 20th century*. It was the book that really put Marcuse on the map. Traditional Marxists and capitalists hated it, but the growing band of young political activists loved it. In the book he attacked the American capitalist society for reducing human beings to consumers at the mercy of advertisers, with their freedom curtailed by the ever-manipulated need to carry on consuming. They are reduced, in his view, to being 'one dimensional' in their thoughts and attitudes. I see nothing fundamentally wrong in this assessment of the wrongs of consumerism, as it's really not the best way of ordering our lives. It's Marcuse's solution that sets him apart from most of his contemporaries.

He offered a new way of looking at the World in his subsequent writings. He was very much for direct action, political propaganda, any means to wake up the people and mobilise them against the forces of capitalism. A later book, *An Essay on Liberation*, was an outline for liberation, for action, for revolution. It was a handbook taken up by a new species of protester that was birthed out of an existing species. Welcome to the *New Left*.

The 'Old Left' were the original political left-wing in the West, such as the Labour Party in the UK. They were typified mainly by the blue-collar workers, the working class, who just wanted a fair wage and food on the table. Out of this movement came the Welfare State in the UK after the Second World War. In general terms their politics didn't travel further than a mutual concern for working people wherever they may be. This is the Labour Party of Kier Hardie, Harold Wilson and Denis Healey and others. Safe, comfortable and traditionally British. This was the party my father voted for, people he – an ordinary working man (taxi driver) – felt were a safe pair of hands to look after his interests. In the USA they were the Democrats, typified by Franklin D Roosevelt and Harry Truman, with a sprinkling of Communists beavering away intent on disruption, particularly through the Unions.

The *New Left* were the angry young upstarts. Not so

interested in economics, but much more interested in the culture of the day. Reminiscent of the changes in Marxism itself, with Marx and the old guard concentrating on economic theory, but with the new guard at the Frankfurt school re-envisioning it in cultural terms. The New Left had less to say about social class and more to say about the issues of the day such as feminism, racism, civil rights, drugs, the environment and the peace movement. In fact, *perhaps they had too much to say?*

Leaders of this political offshoot in the USA included men such as Jerry Rubin and Albert Hoffman, who represented the 'hippie' fringe. Hoffman was quoted thus:

"Once one has experienced LSD, existential revolution, fought the intellectual game-playing of the individual in society, of one's identity, one realizes that action is the only reality; not only reality but morality as well. It exists in the head. I am the Revolution." [1]

British crooner Matt Monro spent time in California in the late 1960s where he recorded what would become a 'battle hymn' of the flower-power generation. Of course many popular songs which emerged in that era were focused on social and political change; not for nothing is the era remembered as that of 'sex, drugs and rock and roll'! Yet in the light of Cultural Marxism, and its subtle mainstreaming during the 1960s and 1970s, the lyrics are of interest, albeit that Matt Monro's song *We're Gonna Change the World* was supposedly a satirical take on the 'women's liberation' movement. The chorus refrain runs: *So, come with us, run with us. We're gonna change your world. You'll be amazed, so full of praise, when we've rearranged your world. We're gonna change your world.* How Monro's song was perceived in

1970, when it was released, is for music historians to recount. Yet as a social comment its chorus sounds like a declaration of revolutionary intent! Cultural Marxism was (is) out to change our World, beyond any order of recognition. Of course not all 'revolutionaries' were drug-fuelled, spiritually confused student dropouts. Those who were into revolution looked overseas and made idols out of Marxist tyrants, whose crimes hadn't quite caught up with them yet, men such as Che Guevara, Fidel Castro and Ho Chi Minh. Certainly the image of Che the revolutionary was probably the defining image of the times, adorning many a student bedroom or t-shirt, the fierce 'freedom fighter' who was, in actuality, a ruthless mass-murderer who ponged a bit (he rarely washed).

The New Left was a 'broad church', a clearing house for young discontents with fire in their bellies or whether they were left-liberal, socialist, or anarchist, whether they were drawn into one of the many offshoot subcultures, such as gay rights or the pacifists at *the Campaign for Nuclear Disarmament* (CND) in the UK (Jeremy Corbyn was active in this as a schoolboy). They were united simply through the new freedom they felt they had been given to protest against the 'Old ways'. In the UK the New Left was pioneered by such men as Stuart Hall (who introduced 'cultural studies' into British colleges), Edward Thompson (one of the prime movers of CND in the 1950s) and Raymond Williams (a Marxist philosopher).

And, at the centre of all this, quietly pulling the strings, either indirectly through his books, or directly through direct action, was Herbert Marcuse, *the acknowledged father of the New Left*. To understand his growing credentials, here is something he wrote in

1968:

"UNDER the conditions prevailing in this country, tolerance does not, and cannot, fulfill the civilizing function attributed to it by the liberal protagonists of democracy, namely, protection of dissent. The progressive historical force of tolerance lies in its extension to those modes and forms of dissent which are not committed to the status quo of society, and not confined to the institutional framework of the established society. Consequently, the idea of tolerance implies the necessity, for the dissenting group or individuals, to become illegitimate if and when the established legitimacy prevents and counteracts the development of dissent. This would be the case not only in a totalitarian society, under a dictatorship, in one-party states, but also in a democracy (representative, parliamentary, or 'direct') where the majority does not result from the development of independent thought and opinion but rather from the monopolistic or oligopolistic administration of public opinion, without terror and (normally) without censorship. In such cases, the majority is self-perpetuating while perpetuating the vested interests which made it a majority. In its very structure this majority is 'closed', petrified; it repels a priori any change other than changes within the system. But this means that the majority is no longer justified in claiming the democratic title of the best guardian of the common interest. And such a majority is all but the opposite of Rousseau's 'general will': it is composed, not of individuals who, in their political functions, have made effective 'abstraction' from their private interests, but, on the contrary, of individuals who have effectively identified their private interests with their political functions. And the representatives of this majority, in ascertaining and executing its will, ascertain and execute the will of the vested interests, which have formed the majority. The ideology of democracy hides its lack of substance."[2]

What a mouthful! You can even imagine this as a concentrated monologue delivered in a dour monotonic tone. A quick scan of it should be sufficient to discern the aggressive distaste he displayed for the capitalist American society that had provided him with a comfortable living. The key year was 1968, when theory became action, when the whole World was rocked, the year of the student protests (just a few months after their 'summer of love', how fickle the youth are!).

These were the young turks of the New Left snarling at the Western World. In May 1968, France was virtually brought to a standstill, with general strikes and occupations of factories and universities. Some politicians actually feared a civil war or revolution and this was said to be a cultural turning point in the country's history. The waves of protests had swept through West Berlin, Rome, London, Paris and many cities in the USA, as well as other places. What exactly were these people, mainly students, protesting about? It was a general old moan and one old leftie, looking back to that year declared, *"suddenly it seemed that the coming together of many different acts of revolt could overturn an exploitative and oppressive society in its totality."*[3]

Exploitative? Oppression? We can sense the presence of a certain old German philosopher here, can't we? During the 1960s and 1970s Herbert Marcuse cheerfully welcomed invitations to speak at many of the centres of protest, the universities. During one particular French student occupation some leaders put on a seminar entitled *'journee marcusienne'*. In Rome placards declared, "Marx, Mao, Marcuse". But there was an even more sinister development here. He was happy to accept invitations to speak ... but insisted that invitations should not be offered to others, particularly those he disagreed with. He said that they can't be allowed to persist in their misguided and evil ways, giving birth to a slogan that is relevant today, *no free speech for fascists*. Out of this idea comes one of the central themes of the political correctness that increasingly plagues us today. Let us investigate ...

Here's how Marcuse thought this through. He began well by admitting that classical virtues such as tolerance and free speech are desirable. But, he says, our society is divided between the oppressors, who have the power and the 'disenfranchised' who have little. So there should be little tolerance extended to the oppressors, but much tolerance extended to 'groups that are being discriminated against'. In his own words he was advocating *"the systematic withdrawal of tolerance towards regressive and repressive opinions."* And who are the purveyors of these opinions? According to Marcuse they were the groups and movements promoting chauvinism, aggressive policies, discrimination on the grounds of race and religion or which oppose the extension of public services, such as social services and medical care. In his view this just about included anyone who didn't share his particular Marxist view of society. This also included restrictions on certain teachings in universities and intolerance of any movements from the 'right-wing', which led to the already-mentioned chant, *no free speech for fascists*.

This is where it gets very sinister, because *who provides the definition of 'a fascist'?* We are reminded of Theodor Adorno's definition, in *The Authoritarian Personality*, endorsed by Marcuse, that *fascism can result from religion and conventional middle-class values on family, sex and society*. Something has been turned on its head here. Marcuse and his ilk are implying that free speech and tolerance are only to be extended to those who *don't fit their particular definition of fascism* – basically anyone who is not from a traditional, middle-class Christian background!

What Marcuse is advocating is to give license to those (loosely) of the New Left to use any tactic they can think of to oppress and repress their opposition, basically those of a Conservative, Judeo-Christian inclination, now renamed 'fascists'. And this could involve direct action, as anything is justified for the self-proclaimed 'social warriors on the side of peace and liberation'.

So, we now have the 'set up', the first seeds of the madness that pervades our Western cultural life. We will next look at the journey between then and now.

NOTES

[1] Quoted in "Fascist Ideology of the Self: Mailer, Rubin and Hoffman" by Armand Barotti, published in Literature & Ideology, No 6, 1970

[2] 1968 postscript to Herbert Marcuse's 1965 essay on "repressive tolerance"

[3] Quoted in "The year the world caught fire" by Chris Harman in 1968, published in Socialist Review, May 2008

Tear it all down!

There is an aspect of our Western culture that has been creeping relentlessly into the 'big picture'. It has been the butt of many jokes in past years and considered a harmless oddity, *but not anymore*. It now rules the roost and it has very sinister intentions. It goes by the name of *political correctness*.

It didn't just pop out of nowhere, as a whim of an over-zealous civil servant. It is the outcome of a 'long march' through recent history and is nothing less than a strategy to undermine and destroy the bedrocks of Western civilisation, the Judeo-Christian framework, with particular emphasis on the traditional family unit. It is the legacy of Marcuse, Adorno and others from the Frankfurt School and it has carried the toxic 'spirit of the 60s' through to the modern day, modifying itself as it does so. It is very much in the spirit of Cultural Marxism, as it takes its core beliefs and assumptions from the Critical Theory insistence on the rejection of the notion of objectivity in knowledge, a rejection of absolute truth.

But this beast has a bite that is fatal. Consider Tim Farron, the political leader of the Liberal Democrats in the UK who was driven out of his job through assumptions about his views on the LGBTIQ+ agenda. Or Walt Tutka, a substitute teacher in the USA who was fired for handing a Bible to a student. Political correctness acquired this bite by worming its agenda into government legislation, and if you are wondering how this can happen then we are going to need a history lesson. How did the counter-culture of the 60s become such a driving force in the culture of today?

The central thrust of Cultural Marxism is the promotion of a 'victim culture', of building a narrative whereby all of the World's ills are the fault of the prevailing culture, specifically white men working from within a Christian context. Critical Theory began to roll out a series of 'causes', centring on those deemed to be 'victims', such as black people, women, homosexuals, native Americans etc. There seems to be a worthiness in this until one realises that these causes were just part of the context of Cultural Marxism. Anyone who dares criticise this process was and are now condemned variously as homophobic, misogynist, Islamophobic, racist, sexist and so on. Most of all – in the legacy of Marcuse – they are labelled as 'fascists'. You may remember the anarchist 'Rick', played by Rick Mayall in the 1990s sitcom 'The Young Ones'. When stuck for words this character, a comedy parody of a young 'new leftie', would scream 'fascist' at whoever was annoying him. This was an ironically accurate depiction of the New Left's reflex response to any criticism of its activities.

So let's reword the gist of that last paragraph, to consolidate its impact. Whereas traditional Marxism set up the ruling class, the 'capitalists', as the aggressors and the working class as the victims, Cultural Marxism takes the same pattern but tweaks it. In place of the ruling class we have the traditional Western 'Christian' society as aggressor and any number of 'marginalised' groups as 'victim'. One key idea here is that the aggressor is never allowed any leeway, any shred of compassion, or any way of redeeming itself. It must be destroyed. Surely we see here the primacy of the ideology rather than a real concern for the 'victims' who are being 'defended'? This may seem a cynical attitude for me to take, but imagine if I am right on this, how cynical it is to perpetrate an ideology that creates conflict for the Cultural Marxists' own ends?!

Now here is something important. We may now have some sort of handle on Cultural Marxism, but what about *Cultural Marxists*, who are they? It is important that we don't judge those caught up in this mindset, the 'victims', as Cultural Marxists, as they are simply actors in the drama. Who, actually, *are pulling the strings?* Who, actually, *are* the Cultural Marxists, those who are setting the agenda and promoting it? A difficult one, as we may never actually find out, though there is probably many a university professor or social commentator, who may fit this bill to a certain extent. We may never find the answer to this question.

So, for Cultural Marxists, a Christian *can never be a victim,* even in the case of the persecuted Church in Muslim countries (is there such a word as Christianophobia?). *Israel and the Jews*, ironically (as Cultural Marxism was an ideology mainly birthed by Jews) and sadly (in that Jews have been history's eternal victims) are not allowed any 'victim' status under this New Left thinking (witness the inability of Jeremy Corbyn to acknowledge, let alone deal with, anti-Semitism in the UK Labour Party at the time of writing, 2018). Similarly, a *white heterosexual male* can also never be a victim. Has anyone heard of men's rights or male emancipation in an age when a feminine spirit seems to be holding ever-increasing sway? Another key idea, equally important, is that the 'victim' is chosen by the Cultural Marxists themselves and held in some sort of hierarchy (with 'multiculturalism' at the top at present). The 'victims' don't get a say in this, unless they themselves are Cultural Marxists, which is unlikely. It is 'Big Brother' gone ... mad, mad, mad!

Out of this, political correctness triumphs and engineers the rise of the 'nanny state' with increasing intrusions and restrictions on the grounds of 'health & safety' to whittle away at our freedoms. This is what the New Left are all about these days and, with particular hold on the media and the metropolitan elite elements of society (the 'chattering classes'), Cultural Marxism is beginning to succeed in its goal of a controlled, collectivist society. McCarthy-ism is never more needed than now, but, unfortunately the horse has already bolted and *ironically* the current 'McCarthy-ists' are those now naming and blaming people who are perceived to have infringed the rights of a member of a 'victim group', even if this infringement had taken place over 20 years ago!

But we need to return to our story to see the developments since Marcuse and his revolting students. We can say that the scene had been set for what came next. Marcuse and others from the Frankfurt School churned up the soil and planted a few seeds. What came next were developments of the 'victim' culture scenario through the appearance of a whole new socio-babble philosophy, *deconstructivism*. Interesting choice of name and very much linked to the ethos behind Critical Theory. It's all about tearing things down. Just as the students created physical havoc in the colleges in 1968, these philosophers were going to do the same with the fabric of Western society.

Before we go further it is worth showing the continuity between the early theories of the 1930s and their first fulfilments in the 1960s. We started with *Critical Theory, a system where everything is there to be criticised and deconstructed.* One basic principle was to *reject the notion of objectivity in knowledge.* This is highly significant and lays down the roots of the relativism that is one of the key drivers in the Western world today and, in fact, the whole of *postmodernism* – the key driver of modern Western culture - flows from this one statement. It answers the question, *what is truth?* with the response ... *whatever you want it to be.* We now have *deconstructivism.* What on earth is that?

There's a new chap in town, an Algerian Jew called *Jacques Derrida.* He is the author of this new idea. To understand this we first need to know what a binary is. We have all been exposed to this word in an unfamiliar context, with the endless discussions on gender identity. In this context everything is born out of conflict, so we can immediately see the Marxist influence here. *Binary* refers to two things in opposition, such as the rich capitalists and the poor workers in Marx's original thinking (before the World got very complicated!). Now, according to Derrida, we can expand this into relationships, where one element is dominating the other, such as the male dominating the female, or the white man dominating the black man. We are now starting to see some of the underlying theory behind the 'victim culture' introduced by Marcuse, with an 'oppressor' and a 'victim'.

In deconstructivism, binaries must be criticised and overthrown, wherever they may be found, even in the great stories in literature, where the original meanings put there by the author are secondary to the 'real meanings' as discerned by the reader/analyst. This is key, particularly when we remember the main tenet of

Critical Theory of rejecting the notion of objectivity in knowledge. In their view, as there is no objective, absolute truth, even words penned by an author (and this includes the Bible) are *there to be re-interpreted by the reader*. This was all introduced by Derrida in 1967 in his books, *Writing and Difference, Speech and Phenomena* and *Of Grammatology*. It has been said that, just as with Critical Theory, deconstructivism is a philosophy *that says nothing*, as it is basically destructive in nature. Without being side-tracked into other areas we need to consider the relevance of all of this in our current discussion.

Deconstructivists want to move us away altogether from binary thinking. So, instead of black and white we have an infinite selection of greys, so that no one colour is dominant enough to prejudice our thinking. 'Man and woman' is too binary, we need to look at the whole spectrum of genetic possibilities! You can start to see the impact this thinking has had on the modern World. Let's turn to two current issues, hopefully now illuminated by what we have learned so far:

Feminism: This seeks to liberate women from the roles that Western society has imposed on them. Of particular abhorrence is the Biblical role model of wife/nurturer.

Gender: 'Queer' theory seeks to deconstruct the traditional binary configuration of male/female. The key assumption is the apparent disconnect between biological sex and perceived gender. They reject the physical biology as irrelevant and take the postmodern view that a person's gender is not absolute, but whatever the person feels it to be.

There was a time when this would have been considered, at best, quirky, if not absolutely bizarre! But times have changed now that Cultural Marxism has embedded itself so deeply into our society. Here's an example of the 'madness' taken from the current news. One of the most watched TV shows is *I'm a Celebrity get me out of here!* with a clutch of 'celebrities' dumped in the Australian jungle for our amusement and entertainment. One such 'celebrity' was the 22-year-old YouTube 'personality' Jack Maynard. After 'entertaining' us for three days in the jungle he was dramatically pulled from the programme. Why? Because six years ago he had used the 'N' word (rhymes with 'trigger') in a tweet (along with a few other minor misdemeanours). It seems that no-one is beyond the clutches of the 'thought police' and anyone can be classed as an 'oppressor' these days, simply by having someone sieving through your past history (admittedly this was instigated by *The Sun* newspaper, purely as a ratings booster). The media is a compliant partner in this toxic atmosphere of blame and consequence and, at the time of writing, is an ever-growing phenomenon.

A telling quote of where we are now supposedly comes from the well-known French philosopher, Voltaire:

"To learn who rules over you, simply find out who you are not allowed to criticize."

It is a brave man (or woman) who dares to test this one out in the current climate.

It's a Mad, Mad, Mad, Mad World

6

There was a quirky star-studded film from gentler times. It was called *It's a Mad, Mad, Mad, Mad World* and was basically a treasure hunt spanning California, with lots of car chases and jolly japes. Yet its title may have been prophetic as the World today is truly mad - and not in a jolly sense. The warning signs may have been the Brexit/Trump 'double whammy', but the liberal and leftist establishment has fought back, with interest, and the average citizen in the West whose mind has not been jellified by overdoses of reality TV, immersive digital entertainment and celebrity trivia must really wonder whether we have slipped into an alternative dimension.

Wasn't there a time where we had a spatial sense of the political climate, when we knew what a far-left-winger was and when someone on the far-right was perhaps missing a few marbles? Both extremes were tolerated and kept within safe zones and far away from our comfortable lives ordered by middle-ground compromise politics. *There they are on the TV news, on their marches, with their abrasive banners and angry faces. Let them let off steam, it's of no relevance to me.*

How times have changed, as the mindset that governs these people has now wheedled itself into the mainstream and is very much affecting us all in different ways. We can blaspheme the Christian God to our heart's content, but we risk our livelihoods if we even hint at the n-word when referring to a black man.

We live in a World where those on the far-left will defend militant Islam, despite the violent disdain offered back. Where the EU has an iron hand to punish 'human rights' crimes within its borders but ignores the most savage atrocities committed just beyond its borders. Where left-wingers would weep and wail over Palestine but ignore Syria, China, Sudan, Zimbabwe, Yemen, North Korea or the Congo. Where the far-left oppose far-right movements as long as they are run by white men, but actually often speak in favour of foreign far-right regimes, as long as they are anti-Western. Where leftist apologists point at the mass murder committed by right-wing dictators but conveniently ignore the far greater numbers killed at the hands of left-wing dictators, such as Stalin or Mao.

It used to be that the right-wing tended to support victims of communism and dictatorships connected to Soviet Russia, whereas the left-wing supported the victims of fascistic regimes and right-wing dictatorships. For the far-left the goalposts have moved, *they would now treat as friend anyone who opposes Western democracy.* That is their over-riding narrative and it ensures that you wouldn't get them marching against Mugabe's Zimbabwe, or the Islamic massacres in Africa, or the murderous Syrian regime, but they would take to the London streets in their droves if the family of a Palestinian suicide bomber was turfed out of their house by the 'evil Zionist regime'. You may remember at the time of the Gulf War that demonstrations were a-plenty against the actions of the Western coalition forces, but you would not see any on the streets in the years leading up to this protesting against the evil genocidal regime of Saddam Hussein. Pic 'n' mix morality, indeed!

Yes, these are extreme views and this comes from the far-left agenda, rather than the more moderate liberals, and it would be unfair to tar the latter with the murky brush of the former. The fact is that there are a myriad of viewpoints about a myriad of things and simple logic is not always followed, though deeply held prejudices tend to hold sway. This highlights the broad spectrum of views that span the political landscape from left to right, these days. *Politics has never been so complicated!*

It is interesting and significant that those people, nominally of the far-left, who embrace the 'Brave New World' ushered in by Cultural Marxism, proclaim themselves as progressives. They consider this homogenising of society and the stripping of individual freedoms as progress. Yet haven't we grown up with this concept, of society's forward trajectory, breaking down barriers and forging ahead, going by the name of 'progress'? We are fed the refrain, this is progress ... *we've turned away from old superstitions / outdated rules of moral conduct / the restrictions of the patriarchal society.* It may be a forward trajectory for them, but for right-minded people (and not just Christians) it is simply a retreat from our true foundations. It is nothing more than a symptom of a civilisation that has run its course and is in the final phase of self-destructive decadence, around the same place that Rome was in before it fell, as we saw in the Introduction.

There is an inconvenient, uncomfortable and unspoken truth here which makes sense to those of a forensic disposition. *There is really no difference between those of the far-left and the far-right, where it really matters.* One may promote internationalism, over the nationalism of the other, *but they both boil down to the masses being controlled and abused by a murderous elite,* whether a Nazi Germany or a Communist World State.

It is a fact that, in terms of how these philosophies have been implemented, there is little difference between Fascism and Communism. They both worked together, usually against the liberal societies of the day, many times in the early to mid-20th Century, with a prime example being the (temporary) pact between Stalin and Hitler. The dark corridors of the human soul stretch out both to the left and to the right and, in the dark, both look pretty much the same. It has all become a blur and the world of politics has given birth to a whole swathe of political denominations, though I doubt if it will ever match the 40,000+ varieties that have sprung forth from the Church. We can begin to appreciate the upheaval in the 2016 USA elections, where the 'finish line' was contested by two candidates seemingly at home in the extreme expressions of their 'wing' of their party, leaving the average citizen having to choose the one who would do the least damage, rather than the one who would actually benefit the Nation. It was a no-win situation for the electorate and it was probably the spark that lit the fires currently raging in American society.

Perhaps the craziest (and saddest) spectacle has been the alliance between the left and the Islamists. The only thing they seem to have in common is their disdain or hatred for the Western culture (and, of course, the Jews) but this seems to outweigh the certainty that, if the Islamists ever succeed in building their caliphate in the UK, the first heads to roll (literally) would be the liberals, leftists, gays, feminists, atheists (and, of course, the Jews). Yet the left-wing can't bring itself to oppose them and would support them on campaigns and marches on whatever issue the Islamists choose. Hatred outweighs everything, it seems, especially when it is dressed up in the language and actions of political correctness. Here is a real-life story to support this sad fact.

It was said to be the biggest child protection scandal in UK history. It was in Rotherham and, incredibly, it went on undetected for over twenty years and involved the systematic sexual abuse of over 1,400, mostly underage white girls, some as young as 12 years old[1]. The gang, who have now been brought to justice, were of Pakistani Muslim origin and it is now being revealed that this may be the tip of a very sordid iceberg, with similar goings-on in other towns in the Midlands and the North of England. The tragedy of this is that it could have been nipped in the bud, but it wasn't, despite the police and the council being very well aware of these activities very early on. At a House of Commons hearing into the case, three main reasons were given why this wasn't dealt with earlier:

1. Community relations – not wanting to be accused of racism, because of the fact that the perpetrators were Asian Muslims.

2. Prejudice and indifference to the victims, who were working-class girls (some in care homes), living on the margins of society.

3. Self-interest – the Labour council didn't want to lose votes from its largely ethnic electorate.

The overriding factor was *political correctness*, where the facade of 'multiculturalism' had to be maintained, despite the connection to Islamic culture that seemed to lie at the very heart of the case. Many of these South Asian young men were trapped in loveless arranged marriages and were taught that 'white girls' were fair game and were to be treated as subhuman. You will get a better flavour of the issues here from a news item, regarding a recent outburst from Labour MP, Naz Shah, a close ally of Jeremy Corbyn. She spoke out against a fellow Labour MP, Sarah Champion, who had remarked that Britain *'had a problem with Pakistani men targeting vulnerable white girls'*. Despite new Pakistani grooming scandals being uncovered in Newcastle and other places, Shah had this to say about her fellow MP, that she used *'blanket racialised, loaded statements that stigmatised the Pakistani community'*. Corbyn, on his Facebook page, praised Shah and accused the newspaper that originally printed Champion's remarks of using *'Nazi-like terminology about a minority community'*.

Can you read between the lines here? Here we have the biggest child abuse scandal ever to happen in the UK and, rather than addressing the root causes of the scandal, the spokespeople of Cultural Marxism attempt to imply that 'victims' can't be perpetrators and anyone who believes otherwise is labelled with words like 'racist' and 'nazi'. Meanwhile there are 1400 young girls with ruined lives and, no doubt, other groups of young men continuing the abuses elsewhere, secure in the (hopefully dwindling) protection of 'victim immunity'.

Here's another shocking example of the toxicity of political correctness. In September 2015 when, in a case against an Asian paedophile, Mr Justice Walker in his appeal judgement affirmed that the original lower court judge had been correct to cite perceived additional harm that Asian girls might suffer within 'their communities' as victims of paedophilia. The UK press (e.g. *The Times* of 18 September 2015) was quick to point out that this potentially created a hierarchy of victims, with Asian girls seen as ranking higher than white girls, and with sentencing adjusted accordingly. The NSPCC was among the chorus of critics of this peculiar judgement. Honour crimes in the UK remain a persistent social problem that has attracted little interest from the 'chattering classes'. Instead in mid-2017 the UK government seemed far more interested in the potential for 'abuse' within UK Sunday Schools, and with the prospect of OFSTED inspectors being required to interview UK Sunday School attendees! Whilst that bizarre plan was shelved in late 2017, it did at least illustrate how Cultural Marxism prioritises what it sees as its enemies.

Where else does political correctness scratch and tear at the fabric of sensible living? Well, certainly at many of those closeted laboratories of skewed thinking, the universities. The University of California is such a place. Students have to be very careful what they say, for fear of offending the 'thought police' (rather than the minorities who are supposedly offended but, in reality, mostly couldn't give a fig!). Here are some no-nos:

"There is only one race, the human race". This is supposedly offensive to 'people of colour' as it 'denies their ethnic experience and history'.

"America is the land of opportunity" implies that 'people of colour' are lazy, incompetent and need to work harder?!

Welcome to the world of *micro-aggressions*. These are casual remarks that you and I may make out of innocence, but which could be taken by others as an offense. These are the triggers that feed the political correctness culture and, despite the claim of ushering in a society suffused with brotherly love, actually creates far more division and strife, by perpetuating a culture of perceived victimhood.

With its accent on 'victims', Cultural Marxism has even convinced some in the University system that they themselves fall into this category, such is the power of this insidious philosophy. A former law student at a major University is suing it for loss of earnings because she wasn't allowed to sit her exams in a private room due to chronic anxiety and, as a result graduated a year later than expected. She is suing for the wages she would have earned in that past year! Other cases abound, including a student who so objected on receiving any kind of criticism that she felt that if she attained any grade lower than a First, it would be the fault of others. The National Union of Students (NUS) has even tried to ban cheering and clapping because it could give anxiety to the more sensitive students. Where on earth has the bulldog spirit gone that made this nation great? Where is the 'stiff upper lip'? Have people basically changed that much in a couple of generations? Probably not, but there seems to be little resistance to the life being sucked out of the current generation through the destructive influence of mind-numbing media, trivia being pumped into our brains ... and the subtle machinations and restrictions to our personal freedoms through political correctness (and its cousin, *health and safety*). Not for nothing, it seems, is the current generation becoming increasingly dubbed "the snowflake generation".

So you now see the mess we in the West are in. Perhaps you are puzzled how this craziness could have crept up on us. Wasn't Communism defeated in the 1980s with the collapse of the Soviet Empire? Hasn't Russia opened up more to the forces of democracy and capitalism? The actual story is very different to what you may have been fed in the media and through academia. This may sound like the mutterings of a conspiracy buff but before you judge me I need to ask a very important question:

What if academia and the media and even Hollywood has fed us *their* version of the truth, rather than the *actual truth?* What I am not saying is that we have to question everything but, in order to test the hypothesis that there may have been some 'spin' to news and events, we have to follow the evidence. If there had been a proven left-wing bias in academia, media and Hollywood since the war, then we must find at least some of the evidence we need.

Academia may provide the death of us all! It was the academics who devised and promoted the subversive objectives of Cultural Marxism, it has been the academics (aka. theologians) who serve to obscure the simple faith in Jesus and it is apparently the Islamic scholars who justify and encourage the nihilistic death-squads through their interpretations of their sacred texts. In 1972 Dr Myron L. Fox ran a series of lectures entitled 'Mathematical Game Theory as applied to Physical Education' to university graduates, who were then asked to rate his performance in a questionnaire. He was marked highly, 80% of them rated him as well organised and who stimulated their thinking. They lived to regret this as the whole thing was a hoax, Fox was an actor who just read out rearranged sentences from a Scientific American article! The talk was full of contradictory statements and double talk but this was all overlooked and their integrity was sacrificed at the altar of the illusion of intellectual authority.

The reason why this is relevant is that our modern politically correct culture is being fed by babbling academics, mainly from American university arts and social studies departments and particularly those who specialise in the latest cultural 'theory', whether it addresses race, agenda, identity or religion. Many have been sucked into the 'Professor's new clothes' and are far too sophisticated to realise that their beloved academic is wandering around butt naked! But this was no joke, because, incredibly, some of this 'theory' eventually became 'practice'. The focus was on elevating victims of past injustices into a position of such dominance that any criticism of this would be met with hostility and alienation. From a (worthy) starting point of addressing victimisation of women, gays and blacks, 'theory' elevated each into a category of its own, that couldn't be criticised or challenged by using universally-held criteria of argument or debate. Each became a narrative of its own, protected by the relativism of the age (what may be right for you may not necessarily be so for me) and to this list was added new categories, such as suicide bombing, Hindu wife burning, feminine circumcision or … the rights of gays to promote their ideologies through the talents of Christian bakers. Those on the outside are not allowed to make judgements as the Cultural Marxist narrative was free to decide what was right or wrong and that no-one else had the right to comment.

If you do happen to clash with this 'narrative' then expect to be smeared by accusations of being a racist, a nazi, a fascist, a homophobe, islamophobe, even an anti-Semite (if it suits the 'narrative'). You will get special attention if you are perceived as a member of the 'imperialistic' class i.e. a white, middle-class male Christian. You will note that there are no 'isms' or 'phobias' to protect anyone who is white, middle-class, male or a Christian! You are an enemy by definition of

Cultural Marxism, unless you join the band of 'useful idiots', a term coined by Lenin, referring to those he and his fellow communists were able to cynically manipulate to further their own ends.

This is the driving force of our politically correct culture ... and it is certainly no joke any more!

NOTES

[1] The full story can be read at
https://en.wikipedia.org/wiki/Rotherham_child_sexual_exploitation_scandal

Wrapping it up

7

Sometimes it can be very revealing to eavesdrop on conversations between people who have some sort of finger on the pulse of what's going on, in the public arena and behind the scenes. Let us have a listen.

First up, a recent podcast from Sam Harris, the celebrated atheist, featuring the conservative commentator and writer, Douglas Murray, who is also the deputy editor of the Spectator magazine. Although neither was coming from a Christian worldview they were nostalgic for the days when there was an acknowledged foundation to our society, the certainties presented by the Judeo-Christian tradition (though they attempted to separate this from *actual* faith in Jesus). They were both mindful of the fact that there does not seem to be the will to defend Western moral and intellectual values and, frankly (and surprisingly) saw no real hope for the future. They commented on an observation of a student from the developing World, who was very pessimistic about life and was wondering about the purpose of it all, as the World wasn't offering much hope.

Harris and Murray were in agreement that secularism may have kept religion at bay but it doesn't provide any positive contribution to an understanding of the meaning of life. The rampant spread of godless Cultural Marxism seems to have emphasised to these atheist intellectuals the total absence of meaning in our society. And they really weren't happy about it. Yet they had nothing to offer in the way of hope. They saw our current epoch of history as an end rather than a beginning and this they found intellectually absolutely fascinating, but it filled them full of foreboding!

Next up was a conversation between David Rubin, an 'alternative' (i.e. not syndicated, but big on YouTube, on 'The Rubin Report') talk show host of a mildly liberal persuasion and Larry Elder, a black conservative radio show presenter. Elder was there to dispel some myths perpetrated by the 'racial discrimination' narrative. For starters, racism is not considered the top priority for the black community, but rather the demise of the family. He traces this back to the social engineering of the 1960s with the economic incentives given to single women families, as an initiative of the left, thus removing an incentive to keep families together.

Particular ire was directed to the USA 'Black lives matter', which he sees as a false narrative, particularly as statistics indicate that 97% of murders of black people are by *other black people*. Others are not allowed to make these observations unless they want to be labelled as racists or fascists, because it diminishes the 'all white people are racist' narrative that reigns supreme. There is a term for this, *cognitive dissonance*. It's where you hold a particular understanding, *or are told to have these understandings*, even though evidence is shouting that you are wrong and you are conflicted. Elder, being black, is expected to follow the usual narrative regarding racism against his people, yet his observations and intellect tell him that it is a false narrative, despite others' pre-conceptions on *how he should be thinking*, calling him an 'Uncle Tom'. The fact is that the number one cause of preventable deaths for young white men are car accidents, but for young black men it is being killed by other blacks!

Larry Elder considers himself one of the biggest threats to the leftist establishment in America, including the media, academia and Hollywood. Because he is black they expect him to act as a victim. But he doesn't buy into this, so they malign him. Who are the racists now? As usual, truth is being skewed by this malign philosophy. There's a political angle to this as Elder has observed that the leftist Democrats haven't won the white vote since 1964, which explains why they are so interested in open borders and easy immigration.

Finally we eavesdrop on Dave Rubin again, this time in conversation with Dennis Prager, a conservative commentator with a hugely popular YouTube show, *PragerU*. After agreeing that the two main enemies of Western civilisation were militant Islam and the far left, then commenting on the restrictive places Universities had become, controlled by the far left without any opposition, they mused on the 'victimhood' culture. Where did it come from? they asked. The left had turned logic on its head, with emotionalism holding front view. Now the world is not divided between good and bad, but rather between rich vs. poor, strong vs. weak and victim vs, victimiser. They were particularly concerned with the indoctrination of young people, dragging them into leftist thought patterns. It was quite a down-beat discussion and an indicator that, especially for those people who have a handle on things, there is an element of despair about the future.

So, we should now appreciate how the past has affected the present, how *Critical Theory* has worked its way seemingly unchecked through history, providing a current climate, popularly known as postmodernism (just another expression of Cultural Marxism), where truth is fluid and pliable, yet some 'versions' of the truth are not to be challenged, reminiscent of Hitler's Germany or Stalin's Russia. I remind you of Voltaire's quote from a few Chapters back:

"To learn who rules over you, simply find out who you are not allowed to criticize".

The penny should have dropped, though many hints have been provided. To remind you, there is no real difference between the 'far-left' (Communism/Marxism) and the 'far-right' (Naziism/Fascism). They are both totalitarian, they both provide a society where the State is run by a small elite who must be obeyed at all costs. There's a book you must read, "The Big Lie" by *Dinesh D'Souza*, where the by-line tells it all, *exposing the Nazi roots of the American left*. When the antifa demonstrate in public 'against the fascists' you are watching a group of people dressed as fascists and behaving as fascists, claiming to be 'fighting the fascists'. They are all the same. Traditional 'right-wing' fascists may model their policies and thoughts on the racism and anti-Semitism of such as the Nazis, but the 'left-wing' fascists use exactly the same methodologies, of violence, suppression of free speech etc. and, arguably, are just as anti-Semitic (despite many of their number being Jewish!)

Here are some items to show a few of the ways that Cultural Marxism has really messed up our World.

Canada passed a new act on May 17th 2016, becoming Law on June 19th 2017. It was Bill C-16, concerning the LGBTIQ+ community, and here is a summary:

The bill is intended to protect individuals from

discrimination within the sphere of federal jurisdiction and from being the targets of hate propaganda, as a consequence of their gender identity or their gender expression. The bill adds "gender identity or expression" to the list of prohibited grounds of discrimination in the Canadian Human Rights Act and the list of characteristics of identifiable groups protected from hate propaganda in the Criminal Code. It also adds that evidence that an offence was motivated by bias, prejudice or hate based on a person's gender identity or expression constitutes an aggravating circumstance for a court to consider when imposing a criminal sentence.

Its implications are highlighted by these observations by Canadian commentator, Ron Gray:

Well, let's look at C-16 in action. Suppose a skinny-as-a-rake girl looks into the mirror and thinks, "Ugh! I'm so FAT!" In such a case, we would probably say that she may be suffering from anorexia nervosa, and should be offered psychotherapy. But if that same girl looks into the mirror and thinks she sees a boy, C-16 says to her, "That's OK, little guy; we're on your side. Be whoever you wanna be!" What's more, if our legislation follows the example of the ukase [edict] issued (unconstitutionally) by President Obama last week, it will soon be illegal for anyone to even suggest that she should seek counselling. No, instead she'll become eligible for massive doses of hormones that are at war with her DNA, and possibly for radical surgery to remove perfectly healthy body parts. Have we lost our minds?[1]

In September 2017, there was this little snippet in the Daily Telegraph:

When 38-year-old Sophie Tanner celebrated her second wedding anniversary earlier this year, there were none of the usual trappings - no flowers or romantic meal for two; no hastily purchased card sealed with a kiss. It's not that her other half is remiss, but that on May 16, 2015, when the PR consultant took her vows on the steps of Brighton's Unitarian Church, the person she swore to cherish for eternity was, well, herself.

Yes, she had married herself. It's called *sologamy* and yet another result of the erosion of family values and a consequence of the corruption of the old certainties in our society. We may baulk at same-sex marriages, but the 'progression' doesn't end there, with people marrying cars, pillows, dolphins, cats, blow up dolls, snakes, goats, even the Eiffel Tower and the Berlin Wall. It is laughable … but so incredibly sad.

There is a dark side to all of this and it was hinted at earlier. The inescapable fact is that virtually every thinker and activist in our story of Cultural Marxism have one thing in common, their *Jewish ancestry*. It's as inexplicable as the grand story of the Jews and their survival over the last 2,000 years. But the fact remains that Marx, Freud, Adorno, Horkheimer, Marcuse, Derrida etc. may have different geographic and social origins, but they were all Jewish, though none of them were traditional God-fearing Jews. The downside of this is the fuel that it provides to those 'authentically' right-wing (fascist) groups who see Jewish hands everywhere in a myriad of conspiracies. There's a website 'Smash Cultural Marxism' that would mirror a lot of what I have been writing, until you visit their 'Usual Suspects' (now there's a euphemism!) page. There you will find scores of articles blaming the Jews for everything from Islamic terrorism to being fifth columnists. As I said earlier, having undesirable bedfellows shouldn't diminish the truth of our story.

So how does all of this affect us now, in 21st century Britain? It's incredible that the fruits of Critical Theory now surround us. Hatred and suspicion has triumphed over love and collaboration. The current Labour party has provided a channel of prejudice, masquerading as tolerance, our future sacrificed on the altar of the very real wrongs of the past. Yet their arch-enemy, the Tories, are in the thrall of the same Cultural Marxism. There is no forgiveness, history has frozen with no possibility of a clean slate. Instead there is just recrimination and restrictions. There is no real hope for our society if Cultural Marxism is allowed to continue unchecked.

NOTES
[1] From https://www.chp.ca/commentary/whats-wrong-with-bill-c-16

Part Two:
What is this madness?

Sinister connections 8

A few days ago I made a discovery that shocked me so much that, for a couple of days, I was actually too paralysed to continue writing. This has never happened to me before, the usual scenario is to have productive days at the computer followed by sleepless and anxious nights mulling things over. But this time was different. Things started falling into place and I started wondering *what on Earth have I just discovered?* This was different to discoveries in earlier books, such as the Greek vs Hebraic mindset or form vs function. This was the discovery of a very troubling connection ...

In the first Chapter I mentioned Alice Bailey, the theosophist and her ten point plan in 1948 to wrench society away from its Christian roots. Here is the full list:

1: Take God and prayer out of the education system.
2: Reduce parental authority over the children.
3: Destroy the traditional Judeo-Christian family structure.
4: Make abortion legal and make it easy.
5: Make divorce easy and legal, free people from the concept of marriage for life.
6: Make homosexuality an alternative lifestyle.
7: Debase art, make it run mad.
8: Use media to promote and change the mindset.
9: Create an interfaith movement.
10: Get governments to make all these [points] law and get the church to endorse these changes.

Seventy years later, we can sadly attest to the fact that this plan has thoroughly worked itself out into the culture that now pervades the Western World.

I then mentioned that the Frankfurt School had a similar plan, though it was never formally described. Without going into gory details it is *basically the same plan*, certainly in terms of the underlying spirit and grand goal to bring down the traditional family structure and the Judeo-Christian framework of society.

In 1900 a small group of Bohemians founded the Monte Verita community on a mountain above Ascona, in Switzerland. It became a focus for what was the first 'hippie' movement in history, attracting anarchists such as Otto Gross (a follower of Sigmund Freud), dancers such as Isadora Duncan, artists, healers and writers such as Herman Hesse, Carl Jung and D.H. Lawrence. They ate veggie and danced naked at sunrise. They promoted the emancipation of women and new ways of exploring the mind, body and spirit. Most of all, they were united by the philosophy of *theosophy*. Here's where it gets interesting as Alice Bailey was a key theosophist and spent some time at Ascona, in a teaching capacity. There seems to be some evidence that Georg Lukács, one of the earlier voices in the Frankfurt School also had a connection with this place, or at least with people who frequented Ascona. In one analysis there was a connection implied by the descriptor, *theosophically inspired Frankfurt School*. This is the source of the shivers down my spine, a connection between the mystical Alice Bailey and her ten point plan to destroy Christianity and the Marxist Frankfurt School and their plan to destroy Christianity. *Spiritual forces married to a godless ideology, both with the same aim.*

FRIGHTENING!

Theosophy, *'divine wisdom'*, is just a modern day version of that old heresy, *Gnosticism*, with an accent on occult mystical experiences and an assertion that there is some truth in all religions, just different paths. To understand its true heart we need to have a quick look at Gnosticism itself. It is an attempt at re-moulding Christianity. This is implied by the name itself, gnosis being the Greek word for 'knowledge'. Gnostics through history have been puffed-up individuals who have boasted 'secret knowledge', who consider themselves as special superior beings who, through these divine secrets, have ascended to a higher level than mere mortals. The problem comes when others also believe that there is value in following these deluded individuals.

So Gnostics, such as Alice Bailey, are forever sampling at the tree of knowledge of good and evil, in their constant search for 'wisdom', to fulfil their own needs. She had a sense of the 'divine', although it was more to do with the mutterings of 'fallen angels' (demons) than any dialogue or leadings from God Himself. But what of Lukács, Adorno, Marcuse and the rest of the Marxists at the Frankfurt School, who had no room for any spirituality, each being hardened atheists? Could they also be following Gnosticism without any spiritual element? Frankly it doesn't matter, as the involvement of Alice Bailey and her occult society brings in sinister elements that ensure that the cultural Marxists are going to have 'unseen help' in their quest to bring down Western civilisation. We don't need to dwell on mechanism, just observe the consequences of a plan that has reached its sinister fulfilment (though there is surely more to come) as we look around at our 21st century World.

If we were to summarise Cultural Marxism into a single word it is this, *liberation*, albeit a false one. Supposedly freeing people from the 'restrictions' of the Judeo-Christian structure of society would make them happy and fulfilled. Womens-Lib(eration), Animal Liberation, Liberation theology and the rest do nothing more than concentrate on conflict rather than resolution and do nothing to ensure a stable society. Taking it further, it is saying that man (and woman) are basically good, but oppressed by external structures, such as church or family, hindering them from reaching their true potential. Interestingly, this parallels a fundamental aspect of Gnosticism, where individuals can *break through into enlightenment* through 'secret knowledge'. Interestingly, in his immensely prophetic book, 1984, George Orwell gives an apt description of the 'Marxist' culture that mirrors the Cultural Marxism of today. He writes, *"In Oceania the prevailing philosophy is called Ingsoc (English Socialism), in Eurasia it is called Neo-Bolshevism and in Eastasia it is called by a Chinese name usually translated as Death-Worship, but perhaps better rendered as Obliteration of the Self"*.

Taking it still further, here are the basic differences in the four positions we have been exposed to so far:

TRADITIONAL MARXISM

Condition: Human beings basically good.

Problem: Not free because of economic oppression (unless you are the oppressor!)

Solution: Liberation through violent conflict to free society from ruling classes.

CULTURAL MARXISM

Condition: Human beings basically good.

Problem: Not free because of cultural oppression (unless you are the oppressor!)

Solution: Liberation through peaceful (?) conflict to free society from Christianity/traditions.

GNOSTICISM

Condition: Human beings basically good.

Problem: Not free because the material world is basically evil.

Solution: Liberation through secret knowledge to attain 'salvation'.

CHRISTIANITY

Condition: Human beings basically evil.

Problem: Not free because of personal sin.

Solution: Liberation through faith in the completed work of Jesus Christ to attain salvation.

The first three of the above are remarkably similar. The fourth flows against the tide. And that is why it is the Number One target, which is no surprise when one considers the real spiritual forces behind the first three scenarios.

Alice Bailey, occultist, said the following: "Promote other faiths to be at par with Christianity, and break this thing about Christianity as being the only way to heaven, by that Christianity will be pulled down and other faiths promoted." She also said "Liberate the people from the confines of this structure. It is oppressive and the family is the core of the nation. If you break the family, you break the nation."

So Cultural Marxism is not just about a few pesky

rules and regulations. It has a stated objective and a spiritual underpinning, so ignore it at your peril! It is important, though, to dig deeper to realise why, in their view, Christianity is such a danger to them.

Think about the question of *sin*. This is of course what separates us from God and it is the fundamental problem of mankind. What is sin? It is doing things our own way, in opposition to the best way that God has for us. I needed to clarify that, because *sin* means something very different to a Cultural Marxist. To them a sinful act would be one where you are oppressing another person or people group. You are not accountable to a higher power who sets absolute standards of conduct, instead you are controlled by those "in authority" – the State – who decide whether you are infringing whatever set of rules they have created. But the important thing to remember, *perhaps the most important thing of all*, is that in the true destructive spirit of Critical Theory, a 'sinful act' is not an act against whatever 'victim group' you may have offended, but rather **an act against the State**. 'The State' has not created these 'victim groups' because it cares for them. Instead it is using this whole process *to wrench society away from its Judeo-Christian foundations*. It is a purely destructive process, with only the appearance of altruism, disguising the true goal of Cultural Marxism.

One important question to consider is whether the Church itself has unsuspectingly bought into the concept of 'victim groups'. How often do we consider ourselves victims of a society that is post-Christian? Yet …

*No, in all these things **we are more than conquerors** through him who loved us. For I am convinced that neither death nor life, neither angels nor demons, neither the present nor the future, nor any powers, neither height nor depth, nor* *anything else in all creation, will be able to separate us from the love of God that is in Christ Jesus our Lord.* (Romans 8:37-39)

Let's get real, we are victors *not victims*, however we may feel at any moment in time, or how the World treats us. Unlike the growing numbers of 'victim groups' we don't need the Marxists to protect us. Our God is far bigger than that! One thing we need to guard against, though, is not to be sucked into the 'victimhood' mentality. Ask God now to bring to mind any issues that may now need to be reconsidered.

In the way the World now works, the whole concept of sin and morality has been redefined. To be truly moral under this 'new order' is to fight for the 'oppressed', to be a *social justice warrior* (SJW), a self-justified caped crusader of the new Marxism. This is a complete rejection of traditional Christian morality, which they say is governed by the malign hierarchies of the traditional family, the rule of law and the work environment. They have set about this task, of deconstructing a worldview that has been around for twenty centuries, with gusto and sinister purpose. They are striving for a new 'normal', with the implication that all that went before was 'abnormal'. They do this by moving us away from *rationalism* (modern World) and towards *emotionalism* (postmodern World). Debate gives way to 'feelings' that are easily manipulated (think how major tragedies quickly become 'sacred cows'). They tell us that we have new freedoms, now that we are wrenched free from traditional morality. Freedom to have abortions, unnatural sex, assisted suicide, euthanasia, unlimited gender choices and the self-inflicted oblivion granted by recreational drug taking. To be a 'sinner' would be to deprive others of these 'potentials'. It's the 1960s with an edge and we are getting closer to it every day.

They feed upon the apathy of most of us in the Western World, our detachment from history and our pre-occupation with ourselves and our individual needs. They aim to transition us into a State-led existence, where they – the Cultural Marxists – will do the thinking for us and decide what is right and wrong, acceptable and unacceptable. *In short, Orwell's 1984.*

So what can we do? In the first instance, it is good to have a Biblical perspective ...

In the Beginning

9

So here we have an atheistic Marxist plan to strike at the heart of the Judeo-Christian structures of society, aided by the dark spiritual impetus of a Gnostic occult group with the same aim. Amazingly they seem to have succeeded so far and we ask why nobody saw it coming? Perhaps being 'hidden in plain sight' made it possible for them to operate just below the surface of what seemed to be fairly predictable historical processes. It is easy to look at the counter-culture of the 1960s just as a venting of a generation spared the horrors of war with too much money to spend and too much energy to expend. It is surely beyond belief that this could have been a Marxist manipulation, orchestrated mainly by the thoughts and deeds of a collection of German Jewish academics. Being unbelievable doesn't make it impossible, though.

We can't wish it away and the best we can do, as Christians, is to try to understand what we have before us and what the Bible may have to teach us to understand it better. If we look beyond the 'victim culture' that seems to be the preferred mechanism of Cultural Marxism we need to see the 'big picture', the ultimate aim of a traditional Marxist state. Apparently there are three aims:

1. To abolish the injustices of a class system.
2. All people should be equal.
3. Ownership of the means of production and land should be by the State, who will administer it fairly

for all.

It's all an unrealistic pipe-dream and every country that has adopted Marxism/Communism has failed to implement any of these goals for the simple reason that *human beings are incapable of creating a fair society*. In fact, two of the most evil regimes in history, that have killed more of their own people than any other, are Stalinist Russia and the China of Mao Tse Tung, both 'Communist States'. In both cases they ended up with the State controlling everything not for the benefit of the people, but rather for those at the top of the pyramid, in a *totalitarian State*. The class system became even more unjust than before and no-one was equal, apart from the 99% who were equal in their poverty. As George Orwell stated in 'Animal Farm', *all animals are equal but some animals are more equal than others.*

So is this where Cultural Marxism is leading? I think not as the only aspect of Karl Marx's original ideas that they wish to implement is for the *State to control the lives of the population*. This is not for the good of the population, but rather because, whether they realise it or not (and most don't as they are atheists), the *whole system is nothing more and nothing less than a rebellion against God*.

We open our Bibles to Genesis 11 to the first generations of the rebooted family of man, descendants of the godly Noah and his sons. The impression is that the whole of mankind is living together as a single group. Perhaps it was the first true 'Marxist state'? One thing that is certain, though, is that it wasn't a situation that God was happy with, particularly when they planned to build a city, with a tower that 'reached to the heavens' in an attempt to *make a name for themselves*. It seemed that they were intent, as a group, to invade

God's territory, to take an initiative that clearly wasn't part of God's plan. In short, they were in *rebellion*. Proof of this attitude comes from the name of the King who supposedly was supervising these efforts, *Nimrod*. He was the great-grandson of Noah and his name translates as 'rebellion'.

Here's what happened next:

But the LORD came down to see the city and the tower the people were building. The LORD said, "If as one people speaking the same language they have begun to do this, then nothing they plan to do will be impossible for them. Come, let us go down and confuse their language so they will not understand each other." (Genesis 11:5-7)

So it seemed that God had originally allowed them to communicate with a single language, to see whether this would work out well. It didn't and it demonstrates the basic inability for mankind to behave itself. God simply couldn't trust them. Living as a single State inclined them towards rebellion towards their Maker, so God had to thwart them by confusing their language.

So the LORD scattered them from there over all the earth, and they stopped building the city. That is why it was called Babel — because there the LORD confused the language of the whole world. From there the LORD scattered them over the face of the whole earth. (Genesis 11:8-9)

So they were scattered and we have the birth of Nations. Globalism is not God's preference whether then or now. The basic rebellion in the human heart remains and the result of globalism – surely the goal of *Marxism* – is rebellion against God on a grand scale. We can only be trusted in smaller groupings, albeit nations, territories, regions or city States. Yet, even then, we are not totally to be trusted.

In the days of Samuel, the people of Israel were ruled by divinely appointed *judges*, people who had the ear of God and who were ideally placed to act on His commands as they weren't distracted by the allure of having to run a Kingdom. Unfortunately this wasn't to continue.

So all the elders of Israel gathered together and came to Samuel at Ramah. They said to him, "You are old, and your sons do not follow your ways; now appoint a king to lead us, such as all the other nations have." (1 Samuel 8:4-5)

They wanted to be like other nations. But, by doing so, they sent out a signal, a bad one.

But when they said, "Give us a king to lead us," this displeased Samuel; so he prayed to the LORD. And the LORD told him: "Listen to all that the people are saying to you; it is not you they have rejected, but they have rejected me as their king. As they have done from the day I brought them up out of Egypt until this day, forsaking me and serving other gods, so they are doing to you. Now listen to them; but warn them solemnly and let them know what the king who will reign over them will claim as his rights." (1 Samuel 8:6-9)

From that point onwards the nation lost its special position as a people ruled directly by God, through His prophets and judges. It became a Kingdom, like any other, people being ruled by an autocrat, who would increasingly want to go his own way, rather than God's Way, as we see with the first King, Saul, and most of the last Kings, particularly those of the Northern Kingdom of Israel.

This may be better than a Global state but it's still not the best arrangement. In fact mankind has yet to find the best way of ruling itself and we look forwards to the only way, a true theocracy, when Jesus rules from Jerusalem in the Millennium. In the meantime we live with the inadequacies of democracies or dictatorships, totally dependent on the moral character of those we choose to rule over us. This is why there can never be a Marxist state. *It may look good on paper but we are simply not capable of running it.* So our conclusion must be that if anyone is edging us closer to an approximation of a Marxist state, it certainly is not God!

We know this is so because of most of our popular end-time scenarios that tend to see the World descending into a totalitarian State, ruled by the *antichrist*. Without pandering to the many conspiracy theories (some of which may actually be true), the setting up of a 'Marxist state' seems to fit the template. Cultural Marxism may very well be Satan's end-time strategy to usher in the antichrist. I am not going to say any more on this, as no doubt your imagination is now running overtime already! Instead, let us draw back from the full picture and have a fresh look at the mechanisms that are working within it.

Cultural Marxism is driven by the creation and policing of a set of random values that have no grounding in truth and are designed to cause conflict and division, with the twin aims of the whittling away of individualism and the growing in dominance of State control. Call me crazy or a scaremonger, but that summary seems to be an accurate pointer as to where things will go if current momentum runs unchecked. Frankly the only power that can counter this is prayer, the kind of prayer that gave us Brexit and Trump, twin roadblocks against the Marxist onslaught. These two 'setbacks' were not just obstacles to a sinister purpose but they helped to clarify the war over hearts and minds that is being fought, particularly for those of us who had no idea that there was such a conflict going on in the first place, something more significant than the petty skirmishes of party politics. The penny dropped when we saw the unbridled hatred on the faces of those 'far-left' demonstrators at anti-Brexit and anti-Trump marches and were reminders of Germany in the 1930s.

Let us remind ourselves of this mechanism. Cultural Marxism is a system which insists that our society is divided into the oppressors and the oppressed. Those *cemented* into the first group are those clinging onto a Judeo-Christian framework, particularly white, male Christians (with Jews – particularly those living in or supporting Israel lumped in as honorary oppressors). Those continuously being added to the second group are those who may have been oppressed (admittedly) in the past and are being encouraged to rise up and fight back (shades of 'workers of the World unite'). There is a third group of those currently in neither group, but the cleverness of Cultural Marxism is that they should live in continual fear of being added to the first group, perhaps through a word spoken in jest, or an inadvisable action or attitude expressed, or any 'perceived sin' against the 'oppressed'.

As I said before, this is all an artificial construct. It's not that some groups are not oppressed, but society now has inbuilt controls to protect these people. Instead we have the relativism of postmodern thinking to create little 'galaxies' within our 'cultural universe', where 'truth' is whatever suits that particular group. It's a denial, of course, of absolute truth and so, as Christians, we can see exactly where this is going.

Strangely enough (though not so for those of you who have read my earlier books) it all goes back to our friends, the Greek philosophers Plato and Aristotle, particularly the latter. Plato was more into objectivity, actual truths. For him, the highest truth, or the *highest good*, was his concept of God, though he is not as Christians know Him to be. Aristotle didn't go with this, with the possibility of many truths, each depending on the 'nature', or feelings, or emotional state of the truth-seeker. For him there was no single truth about anything, but many interpretations of the truth depending on your viewpoint. This may be a simplistic explanation but one can now see how postmodern thinking has fed from this tradition, where *your truth may be right for you, my truth is right for me ... and never the 'twain shall meet.*

Of course we know this to be false, because we follow God's Word, not the musings of an ancient pagan philosopher, however clever he was. At the centre of our thinking is this simple yet profound statement:

Jesus answered, "I am the way and the truth and the life. No one comes to the Father except through me." (John 14:6)

It doesn't get any clearer than that. Jesus is the Truth. What does that mean? At the most basic level it compels us to learn more about what Jesus said and did and take that as our benchmark. We are undoubtedly living in a post-Jesus era, but that shouldn't stop us. Rather than following a set of rules, such as the Ten Commandments, we see, through the life of Jesus, these rules in action, with practical examples that we can apply to our own lives. We will see more of these in the next section.

So we can now see the conflict between the traditional Christian view that has driven our Western society until around the 1960s and the 'progressive' view of the Cultural Marxists that is waging an open war for hearts and minds. It is a war centred on that age-old question, asked by Pontius Pilate, when faced by that angry manipulated mob in Jerusalem.

What is truth?

So you should now have a good idea of the scale of the problem, if you indeed see it as a problem. If this were a book for general consumption then I would slap on a summary and that would be that. It's an unsettling tale and is there really anything we can do to upset the tide? In the words of Private Fraser of Dad's Army, *we're all doomed! DOOMED!*

But ... for Christians ... this is just the beginning of the story.

Part Three:
Dealing with the madness

The times they are a-changin'

10

The genesis of this book was a single Chapter in *Livin' the Life*, that reminded us of the reality of the two Kingdoms. **The Kingdom of God**, inhabited by followers of Jesus:

"They are not of the world, even as I am not of it. Sanctify them by the truth; your word is truth. As you sent me into the world, I have sent them into the world." (John 17:18-19)

And the **Kingdom of the World**, lived in by everyone, though Christians are *"in it but not of it"*. Jesus said, *"My kingdom is not of this world."* (John 18:36)

The central thought regarding our stance as Christians is that we are not called to fix the Kingdom of the World, instead our role should be in the execution of the Great Commission, in helping to rescue people from this Kingdom by guiding them into the Kingdom of God.

Until recently, this activity has been allowed to happen without too much hindrance from our society. Not so now. And there's a *huge* story to be told here, one that is rarely told, particularly in Christian circles. Until now.

It is time now to move from problem to solutions. We hear increasingly of Christians thwarted in their witness by the application of legislation moulded by Cultural Marxism. Refusing to bake cakes promoting gay marriage, or witnessing to work colleagues, or even displaying Bible verses in the workplace are now punishable through a legal system that was originally founded on Biblical principles.

So how do we fulfil the Great Commission in a society that is creating an increasing number of legal barriers to stop us? Simple really.

"... the one who is in you is greater than the one who is in the world." (1 John 4:4)

"The LORD has established his throne in heaven, and his kingdom rules over all." (Psalm 103:19)

The World does not belong to the Cultural Marxists and the P.C.Police. God, in His mysterious way, has simply granted a time for them to have a measure of influence. This is not going to stop Him in any way from building His Kingdom, however defeated we ourselves may feel at the present time. We just need to adjust to changing times. After all, we are not just another 'victim group'. It is *focus* that we need.

The focus we need is on God Himself. When we are confronted with a witnessing situation we must pray for Godly wisdom but we must *also learn to see others as God sees them.*

*"The Lord is not slow in keeping his promise, as some understand slowness. Instead he is patient with you, **not wanting anyone to perish, but everyone to come to repentance**."* (2 Peter 3:9)

This includes the black-cladded Muslim lady, or the gender-confused, or Richard Dawkins himself. We see an impossible target, where we may not have the right words or the courage to engage, but God sees *a lost soul desperate for reconciliation with their Maker, whether they realise it or not.*

God will finish what He has started with anyone He may put in your path. It is your job to discern what your role may be in this process. Remember, He has not left us alone in this enterprise.

"But the Advocate, the Holy Spirit, whom the Father will send in my name, will teach you all things and will remind you of everything I have said to you." (John 14:26)

Arguably, the more persecution there has been, the more authentic will be the Christianity. In recent years our expressions of God's Kingdom in the West has been muffled by the comforts of our materialistic society. We may preach against it and treat it with disdain, but it has fed us, clothed us and entertained us for longer than is actually healthy for us. We have descended into a sloth-like funk and, to be honest, have really been in need of the current crisis to drag us out of it and kick-start some sort of spiritual purpose into us. We may have found our rallying-point, finally a whiff of persecution that we once read about in tales of yonder lands and earlier days. It may energise us and give us some very real purpose, allowing God finally to act supernaturally in our lives, but *it ain't gonna be pretty!*

Although Cultural Marxism has been creeping up into the mainstream for some years, I believe things accelerated in 2016 with the twin 'shocks' of Brexit and Trump, both bitter blows to the liberal establishment (including much of the Church) and setbacks to the 'masterplan'. Both, I believe, came about through serious prayer by serious people, who had the foresight to know, if not necessarily to express, the dangers of Europe and Hillary Clinton. Their spiritual antenna was perhaps telling them that the World was becoming a different place and it was time they motivated themselves into doing something about it.

The times they are a-changin', warbled Bob Dylan, little

realising how the changes he experienced at the time of writing his song were going to make such an impact fifty years later. The lyrics are incredibly prophetic in regard to what we are discovering together in this book. *For the loser now will be later to win ... come mothers and fathers ... your sons and your daughters ... are beyond your command.*

Now straight to the point. At the time of Dylan, the Church failed to respond, stunned into awkward silence and grinding inertia by the *changin' times.* We are now, fifty years later, in a World where the ideas birthed in the 60s as counter-culture, are very much now embedded in our culture, and are even enforced by law. How has the Church responded to these *changin' times?* How have Christians adapted to the very different World in which we find ourselves? We may have timeless truths, but we live in ... sorry to overuse a phrase ... CHANGIN' TIMES and didn't Jesus say:

"I am sending you out like sheep among wolves. Therefore be as shrewd as snakes and as innocent as doves." (Matthew 10:16)

What worked in the 1950s in a nation clinging to the coat-tails of a Christian worldview will not necessarily do the business in our current post-Christian age. Sometimes we fail to notice this as we tend to operate in a holy bubble constructed by the traditions of Church history and coloured by the hues and tones of denominational brushstrokes. Occasionally we venture out to conduct our evangelism, drawing new converts through the walls of the bubble but, if truth be told, many are bouncing back. This is either because the 'new life' we offer is little different from the World from which we have rescued them, or apparently so different as to be irrelevant to their needs or understanding.

Are we as shrewd as snakes, challenging our generation in ways it can understand, always relevant to the questions they are currently asking? Are we as innocent as doves, holding fast to the uncompromised truths as laid down in the Word of God, despite the carping of social commentators who tell us that the Bible is an ancient irrelevance or the chirping of liberal Christians who tell us that the Bible contains only some truth (and even more if we tweak it a bit according to modern interpretations)?

Can the gospel be understood by a culture infected by Marxist poison and driven by a plethora of humanistic forces re-birthed from ancient Athens? *The content of the gospel never changes, but its delivery has to.* This is why Peter used religious language when speaking to Jews in Jerusalem in Acts 2 and Paul used the language of philosophy to the Greeks in Athens in Acts 17. Horses for courses.

I am not saying that all of our evangelists are using the 'language of the pulpit' in their witness to the World (though some do, particularly those with megaphones or who post social media comments IN CAPITAL LETTERS!) This is not about language, this is about something one step back, this is about worldview. Before I explain further, here are some examples from recent history, that highlight our unique problems in trying to be a Christian witness in the West.

Tim Farron, the leader of the UK Liberal Democrats felt he had to resign as *'remaining faithful to Christ was incompatible with being party leader'*. If anything is a sign that our society is 'Post Christian' then this was it. Stanley Baldwin, William Gladstone and Margaret Thatcher (to name but three) certainly had no problems on that front, but they were living in less problematic times.

Ian Sleeper, a Christian restaurant owner, was arrested outside Southwark cathedral for displaying a placard declaring his love for Muslims but hate for Islam and kept in a cell for 13 hours, though eventually not charged with any crime. Dale McAlpine, a street preacher, was arrested in Workington and placed in a cell for telling a passer-by that homosexuality 'is a sin in the eye of God'. In both of these cases Biblical truth resulted in a stay in a jail cell, a tradition very much in keeping with Biblical history, as we are reminded by the adventures of Peter and Paul in Acts. Yet neither case would have fetched such an outcome even just a few years ago. *But times, they are a-changin'*. It is likely, as more evangelists, filled with zeal for their Lord, take to the streets, that this is going to accelerate, with outcomes more serious than a few hours in a jail cell.

It may be that this will be the form of persecution that many have been predicting for Christian witness in our society. Or maybe not …

Following the Master 11

Perhaps we need to change? Perhaps it's a matter of worldview and mindsets? Perhaps there's something to be said for the 'old wineskins'? A brief history lesson is needed to bring you up to speed, if you haven't already read it earlier in my books. Here is a summary from *To Life!*:

Here is a short review of the damage done to the pure gospel of Jesus Christ as a result of Greek thinking infiltrating the Church.

Plato introduced the idea of dualism into the Church, the idea that the physical universe/nature is bad and the spiritual universe/nature is good. Out of this came a whole menagerie of cults and heresies, some still with us today and even present within the thinking of some mainstream denominations. Plato's tentacles are far reaching and adaptive, affecting our view of God and Jesus, the way that we worship and particularly the way we interpret Holy Scripture.

Aristotle seemed harmless, even a positive influence. After all, didn't he just encourage us to think? He did, but he tempted us into thinking dangerous thoughts. The blame was not on him, after all he never claimed to have godly wisdom, but those Christian philosophers and leaders of the medieval Church who claimed divine license and felt free to allow these dangerous thoughts to break through the shackles of godly wisdom. It was now acceptable to use our rational minds to analyse and dissect the Word of God, without any acknowledgement that Holy Scripture is, first and foremost, God's revealed Word to mankind.

Plato, through the teaching of Augustine, introduced such deviations as the clergy/laity divide and Church hierarchies. It also gave licence, through the use of allegory and the 'spiritualisation' of the text, for teachers to read their own ideas and prejudices into their interpretation of Holy Scripture, relegating God to the role of rubber-stamper for such aberrations as antisemitism, persecution of 'other' Christians, religious war, slavery and prejudice against women.

The influence of Aristotle, largely through the teachings of Thomas Aquinas, led to a Christianity that was man-centred, driven by rationalism, rather than God-centred, underpinned by faith in God. What started out as a synthesis of faith and reason, led to the gradual loosening of God's certainties on the human heart, affecting doctrines and practices and producing a faith diluted through compromise.

To summarise, let me repeat one of the final thoughts in *Livin' the Life*:

"We cannot over-stress the influence of Greek thought on Western civilisation and, by extension, on the Western Church. It's amazing to trace so much that we say, think and do to a group of Greek philosophers over two thousand years ago. The Greeks gave us our man-centred view of the world, governed by our intellect and senses. They gave us personal ambition expressed as the individualism that drives our society. They gave us form over function, where we celebrate people and possessions, rather than the actions and purposes they represent. They present us

with a world where God is marginalised, Jesus is no role model and the Holy Spirit is supplanted by just about every other spirit that lurks out there."

Our current Church in the West is dominated, as is Western society in general, by this kind of Greek thinking. This is what drives the way we do our evangelism, youth work, worship, church services etc. etc. It doesn't mean that we are displeasing God by the way we do these things, it just opens up possibilities for other ways, for those who are open for something that is new ... and is also old! *Hebraic thinking.*

And what is the best way to get to the heart of Hebraic thinking? Well, Jesus himself, of course. We will start by examining how he dealt with those who opposed him and who were looking for ways to marginalise him, or worse.

There's another reason for shifting the focus back to Jesus. In the context of the unfolding story in this book, it has been a bitter pill to swallow, to see how a godless philosophy has effortlessly made so many inroads into our society. It is a powerful indictment of the Church not to have seen it coming and, now that Cultural Marxism is beginning to flex its muscles, to have little power, know-how or intent to mount any sort of defence against it. In fact much of the Church, certainly the 'institutional variety' has, to a certain extent, embraced these uncomfortable new realities. It is a worldly Church that does this, not a Kingdom Church. There is a difference. So, at this point in our story, we really need a *taste of the Kingdom*, just as a reminder ...

So, over we go to Jesus in the Gospels and how he dealt with the 'Kingdom' of his day.

Naming and shaming

One method Jesus used was to remind his accusers of their own Holy Scriptures and how these are consistent with his actions.

When the Pharisees saw this, they asked his disciples, "Why does your teacher eat with tax collectors and sinners?" On hearing this, Jesus said, "It is not the healthy who need a doctor, but the sick. But go and learn what this means: 'I desire mercy, not sacrifice.' For I have not come to call the righteous, but sinners." (Matthew 9:11-13)

Here he was condemning their self-importance and even suggesting that, despite their great learning, he wasn't particularly interested in them. What this teaches us is not to be afraid of the academics and eggheads of this World with their clever arguments and arrogant attitudes. Here is another example of the same point.

At that time Jesus went through the grainfields on the Sabbath. His disciples were hungry and began to pick some heads of grain and eat them. When the Pharisees saw this, they said to him, "Look! Your disciples are doing what is unlawful on the Sabbath." He answered, "Haven't you read what David did when he and his companions were hungry? He entered the house of God, and he and his companions ate the consecrated bread—which was not lawful for them to do, but only for the priests. Or haven't you read in the Law that the priests on Sabbath duty in the temple desecrate the Sabbath and yet are innocent? I tell you that something greater than the temple is here. If you had known what these words mean, 'I desire mercy, not sacrifice,' you would not have condemned the innocent. For the Son of Man is Lord of the Sabbath." (Matthew 12:1-8)

Again he stresses mercy over sacrifice. The needs of needy people take priority. When confronted with someone intent on tying you up in knots, perhaps boasting of their 'great learning' to impress onlookers, you need some stock phrases to knock them off their self-designated perch.

The very next episode continues the theme.

Going on from that place, he went into their synagogue, and a man with a shriveled hand was there. Looking for a reason to bring charges against Jesus, they asked him, "Is it lawful to heal on the Sabbath?" He said to them, "If any of you has a sheep and it falls into a pit on the Sabbath, will you not take hold of it and lift it out? How much more valuable is a person than a sheep! Therefore it is lawful to do good on the Sabbath." Then he said to the man, "Stretch out your hand." So he stretched it out and it was completely restored, just as sound as the other. (Matthew 12:9-13)

Jesus came for *people* not traditions. Yet again he shamed the 'opinion-formers' and there were going to be consequences. We find this in the very next verse:

But the Pharisees went out and plotted how they might kill Jesus. (Matthew 12:14)

Arrogant people don't like being made fools of. Revenge is often a consequence, if they are not given an opportunity to save face. Jesus was relentless in his condemnation of these people and he knew very well what the ultimate consequence was going to be. We need to consider this very carefully. Choose your enemies and your battles. It may be worth holding your tongue in some instances, to play the long game, to ensure you can live to fight another day, if your adversary here is someone you expect to meet again.

Condemnation!

Sometimes it can go further.

Then they brought him a demon-possessed man who was blind and mute, and Jesus healed him, so that he could both talk and see. All the people were astonished and said, "Could this be the Son of David?" But when the Pharisees heard this, they said, "It is only by Beelzebul, the prince of demons, that this fellow drives out demons." Jesus knew their thoughts and said to them, "Every kingdom divided against itself will be ruined, and every city or household divided against itself will not stand. If Satan drives out Satan, he is divided against himself. How then can his kingdom stand? And if I drive out demons by Beelzebul, by whom do your people drive them out? So then, they will be your judges. But if it is by the Spirit of God that I drive out demons, then the kingdom of God has come upon you. "Or again, how can anyone enter a strong man's house and carry off his possessions unless he first ties up the strong man? Then he can plunder his house. "Whoever is not with me is against me, and whoever does not gather with me scatters. And so I tell you, every kind of sin and slander can be forgiven, but blasphemy against the Spirit will not be forgiven. Anyone who speaks a word against the Son of Man will be forgiven, but anyone who speaks against the Holy Spirit will not be forgiven, either in this age or in the age to come. (Matthew 12:22-32)

Jesus was unique. After all he was the Son of God. He was in a perfectly justified position of condemning those who just went too far. We are given similar authority but we need to use it wisely. When we don't do this, we land in trouble with the authorities, something that is becoming increasingly common when traditional evangelists demonstrate language and attitudes that may have been applicable in an earlier age, but which now grate against the new politically correct status quo.

Christians are stereotyped as judgemental people, something that doesn't always go down well in polite society. In earlier times this has gone no further than to label us as 'prejudiced', but these days this can land us in a prison cell.

Frankly, it just doesn't work anymore. The need for preaching still remains, but we are no longer a society that responds to judgement with repentance. Rather we are a people who would respond with indignation, violence and law suits. Our 'victim' culture has provided us with a very thin shell, easily broken. If people perceive that *their human rights are being infringed*, even if the infringement is just a shouty preacher with a megaphone. *Especially so*, in the current anti-Christian climate!

Perhaps the greatest put-down in history was dealt out by Jesus to the religious leaders who were intent on condemning both a woman caught in adultery and Jesus himself. Let's remind ourselves:

The teachers of the law and the Pharisees brought in a woman caught in adultery. They made her stand before the group and said to Jesus, "Teacher, this woman was caught in the act of adultery. In the Law Moses commanded us to stone such women. Now what do you say?" They were using this question as a trap, in order to have a basis for accusing him.

But Jesus bent down and started to write on the ground with his finger. When they kept on questioning him, he straightened up and said to them, "Let any one of you who is without sin be the first to throw a stone at her." Again he stooped down and wrote on the ground. At this, those who heard began to go away one at a time, the older ones first, until only Jesus was left, with the woman still standing there. Jesus straightened up and asked her, "Woman, where are they? Has no one condemned you?" "No one, sir," she said. "Then neither do I condemn you," Jesus declared. "Go now and leave your life of sin." (John 8:3-11)

Let any of you who is without sin! Wow, what an answer. Think how this could be used against our fallible judges, politicians, policemen, in fact any of us who are happy to point the finger at others, oblivious of Jesus's own finger pointing back at them (and at the ground), particularly when some of them may be guilty of the very same sin as those they are judging!

Returning to the events depicted in Matthew, the teachers of the Law again pestered Jesus:

Then some of the Pharisees and teachers of the law said to him, "Teacher, we want to see a sign from you." He answered, "A wicked and adulterous generation asks for a sign! But none will be given it except the sign of the prophet Jonah." (Matthew 12:38-39)

They did the same a little later on and Jesus qualified the statement just made by mocking the teachers that they could read the sky for weather signs but they did not have the spiritual discernment to read the signs of the times (Matthew 16:1-4). Of course people we meet are very unlikely to have any kind of spiritual discernment unless it is from the wrong kind of spirit. And in our case, when we are called to preach 'in and out of season', signs may well be necessary.

Signs and wonders

Here is a familiar story.

A few days later, when Jesus again entered Capernaum, the people heard that he had come home. They gathered in such large numbers that there was no room left, not even outside the door, and he preached the word to them. Some men came, bringing to him a paralyzed man, carried by four of them. Since they could not get him to Jesus because of the crowd, they made an opening in the roof above Jesus by digging through it and then lowered the mat the man was lying on. When Jesus saw their faith, he said to the paralyzed man, "Son, your sins are forgiven." Now some teachers of the law were sitting there, thinking to themselves, "Why does this fellow talk like that? He's blaspheming! Who can forgive sins but God alone?" (Mark 2:1-7)

So here Jesus shows his credentials, but he hasn't yet backed them up.

Immediately Jesus knew in his spirit that this was what they were thinking in their hearts, and he said to them, "Why are you thinking these things? Which is easier: to say to this paralyzed man, 'Your sins are forgiven,' or to say, 'Get up, take your mat and walk'? But I want you to know that the Son of Man has authority on earth to forgive sins." So he said to the man, "I tell you, get up, take your mat and go home." He got up, took his mat and walked out in full view of them all. This amazed everyone and they praised God, saying, "We have never seen anything like this!" (Mark 2:8-12)

Now He has backed them up. It was easy for him, of course. His miracles and healings were 100% guaranteed. Not so much for us, though that should not stop us from trying. The reason we should persevere is that the best witness to the world are the mighty deeds of a supernatural God and the perfect faith we show when we act in boldness.

State of the heart

Here is a key little passage:

"No one can serve two masters. Either you will hate the one

and love the other, or you will be devoted to the one and despise
the other. You cannot serve both God and money." The
Pharisees, who loved money, heard all this and were sneering
at Jesus. He said to them, "You are the ones who justify
yourselves in the eyes of others, but God knows your hearts.
What people value highly is detestable in God's sight."
(Luke 16:13-15)

God knew their hearts. He knows our hearts. He also
knows the hearts of everyone you are going to meet. We
all need to be prepared to realise that there are some
things we do, perhaps even things that are held in high
esteem by this fallen World, *that God finds detestable*. This
is especially so in the case of many people you come up
against. How do we tell them this truth without
provoking abuse or violence (or both)? Jesus was
fearless. He always knew what to say, even if the words
were hard and provocative. He was connected to the
Spirit and always knew when to speak and when to
stay silent. We need to pray about this too, because
every situation you come across will be different. There
will indeed be occasions when you are called to speak
boldly and 'call a spade a spade', but these will be
exceptions and getting it wrong can have dire
consequences, as mentioned earlier.

Yet, however you deal with it, this fallen World still
values highly things that are detestable in God's eyes
and there needs to be some way that we can
communicate this to the unsaved, for the sake of their
soul. This will be discussed later on.

Authority

There are an awful lot of competing voices out there.
There's a crowded marketplace for opinions these days,
exacerbated by the online universe of blogs, vlogs and

social media and further strangled by the pesky phenomenon of fake news.

The question is ... who can we believe? Where does the objective truth lie? In a postmodern age of relativism, where 'truth' is bendable and subjective, surely any open heart must be yearning for a trusted source to make sense of everything?

Christians have that source, but we are not the best communicators of it. We know that our source is faithful and true because Jesus has the authority, as the Son of God. But, nonetheless, he still had to explain this to his contemporaries.

Jesus entered the temple courts, and, while he was teaching, the chief priests and the elders of the people came to him. "By what authority are you doing these things?" they asked. "And who gave you this authority?" Jesus replied, "I will also ask you one question. If you answer me, I will tell you by what authority I am doing these things. John's baptism—where did it come from? Was it from heaven, or of human origin?" They discussed it among themselves and said, "If we say, 'From heaven,' he will ask, 'Then why didn't you believe him?' But if we say, 'Of human origin'—we are afraid of the people, for they all hold that John was a prophet." So they answered Jesus, "We don't know." Then he said, "Neither will I tell you by what authority I am doing these things." (Matthew 21:23-27)

This is interesting. In a sense Jesus has already shown his authority with the kind of miracles and healings he had performed (for example, the healing of the leper) and the episode with the paralysed man, where he demonstrated his authority to forgive sins. But the priests and elders weren't satisfied, so they wished to trap him. Instead he trapped them. He answered their question with one of his own and immediately 'put them on the back foot'. Rather than answering them directly and hence allowing them to control the narrative of his final days, Jesus asked them a question that immediately silenced them through their inability to answer it. And because they couldn't answer his question ... he didn't answer theirs.

This is a useful technique, which Jesus also used when asked about paying taxes:

Keeping a close watch on him, they sent spies, who pretended to be sincere. They hoped to catch Jesus in something he said, so that they might hand him over to the power and authority of the governor. So the spies questioned him: "Teacher, we know that you speak and teach what is right, and that you do not show partiality but teach the way of God in accordance with the truth. Is it right for us to pay taxes to Caesar or not?" He saw through their duplicity and said to them, "Show me a denarius. Whose image and inscription are on it?" "Caesar's," they replied. He said to them, "Then give back to Caesar what is Caesar's, and to God what is God's." They were unable to trap him in what he had said there in public. And astonished by his answer, they became silent. (Luke 20:20-26)

Questions, questions

This was so effective for Jesus and it would be so for us ... if we had the wisdom and training to use this method in dealings with others. Here's an example of mind and spirit potentially working together. The mind has to be shrewd enough to latch onto some aspect of the person's life and it may well be that the Spirit is going to have to reveal this to you supernaturally. Once we have reached the starting point, we then have the tricky bit ... of application. This will need to come from God, as *Godly wisdom* will be needed to find the right words to say that is going to convict their heart.

Let's follow one of the dialogues Jesus had with his detractors. You will find this in John 8:13-58.

The Pharisees challenged him, "Here you are, appearing as your own witness; your testimony is not valid." Jesus answered, "Even if I testify on my own behalf, my testimony is valid, for I know where I came from and where I am going. But you have no idea where I come from or where I am going. You judge by human standards; I pass judgment on no one. But if I do judge, my decisions are true, because I am not alone. I stand with the Father, who sent me. In your own Law it is written that the testimony of two witnesses is true. I am one who testifies for myself; my other witness is the Father, who sent me."

His opening salvo is characterised by one word, boldness. He is declaring God, rather than man, as his witness. He is also claiming to be sent by God.

Then they asked him, "Where is your father?" "You do not know me or my Father," Jesus replied. "If you knew me, you would know my Father also." He spoke these words while teaching in the temple courts near the place where the offerings were put. Yet no one seized him, because his hour had not yet come.

Jesus could have trapped himself here with this assertion but he had knowledge that his opponents didn't have – supernatural knowledge – that his time hadn't quite come yet.

Once more Jesus said to them, "I am going away, and you will look for me, and you will die in your sin. Where I go, you cannot come." This made the Jews ask, "Will he kill himself? Is that why he says, 'Where I go, you cannot come'?"

They hadn't yet grasped the supernatural aspect of his mission, so he explains further ...

But he continued, "You are from below; I am from above. You are of this world; I am not of this world. I told you that you would die in your sins; if you do not believe that I am he, you will indeed die in your sins."

He was now declaring more about his identity and his opponents were ready to react accordingly. So they asked him the question that might just condemn him; *"Who are you?"* they asked.

Well, it could have condemned him, had he answered directly.

Just what I have been telling you from the beginning," Jesus replied. "I have much to say in judgment of you. But he who sent me is trustworthy, and what I have heard from him I tell the world." They did not understand that he was telling them about his Father.

Jesus had confused them even more. Now was the time to speak more directly:

So Jesus said, "When you have lifted up the Son of Man, then you will know that I am he and that I do nothing on my own but speak just what the Father has taught me. The one who sent me is with me; he has not left me alone, for I always do what pleases him." Even as he spoke, many believed in him.

The penny had dropped with some of them, so his next statement was addressed to them.

To the Jews who had believed him, Jesus said, "If you hold to my teaching, you are really my disciples. Then you will know the truth, and the truth will set you free."

The rest were peeved and indignant.

They answered him, "We are Abraham's descendants and have never been slaves of anyone. How can you say that we shall be set free?" Jesus replied, "Very truly I tell you, everyone who sins is a slave to sin. Now a slave has no permanent place in the family, but a son belongs to it forever. So if the Son sets you free, you will be free indeed. I know that you are Abraham's descendants. Yet you are looking for a way to kill me, because you have no room for my word. I am telling you what I have seen in the Father's presence, and you are doing what you have heard from your father."

They did what all proud people do. *Don't you know who we are?* was the cry. *Yes, I do ... and it makes absolutely no difference to me who you are. You are all slaves to sin whatever your lineage may be.*

"Abraham is our father," they answered. *"If you were Abraham's children,"* said Jesus, *"then you would do what Abraham did. As it is, you are looking for a way to kill me, a man who has told you the truth that I heard from God. Abraham did not do such things. You are doing the works of your own father."*

Jesus had turned it round and declared that if they were true to their forefather, Abraham, they would never be doing what they are doing now.

"We are not illegitimate children," they protested. *"The only Father we have is God himself."* Jesus said to them, *"If God were your Father, you would love me, for I have come here from God. I have not come on my own; God sent me. Why is my language not clear to you? Because you are unable to hear what I say."*

They are clearly on the defensive and appeal to a higher authority, the highest authority of all. It does them no good because Jesus now goes on the attack.

"You belong to your father, the devil, and you want to carry out your father's desires. He was a murderer from the beginning, not holding to the truth, for there is no truth in him. When he lies, he speaks his native language, for he is a liar and

the father of lies. Yet because I tell the truth, you do not believe me! Can any of you prove me guilty of sin? If I am telling the truth, why don't you believe me? Whoever belongs to God hears what God says. The reason you do not hear is that you do not belong to God."

That must have sent them reeling. So it all starts to get really nasty.

The Jews answered him, "Aren't we right in saying that you are a Samaritan and demon-possessed?" "I am not possessed by a demon," said Jesus, "but I honor my Father and you dishonor me. I am not seeking glory for myself; but there is one who seeks it, and he is the judge. Very truly I tell you, whoever obeys my word will never see death." At this they exclaimed, "Now we know that you are demon-possessed! Abraham died and so did the prophets, yet you say that whoever obeys your word will never taste death. Are you greater than our father Abraham? He died, and so did the prophets. Who do you think you are?"

After the insults came the question again. *Who is this before us?*

Jesus replied, "If I glorify myself, my glory means nothing. My Father, whom you claim as your God, is the one who glorifies me. Though you do not know him, I know him. If I said I did not, I would be a liar like you, but I do know him and obey his word. Your father Abraham rejoiced at the thought of seeing my day; he saw it and was glad."

He had begun to answer them, but they thought they now had him trapped ...

"You are not yet fifty years old," they said to him, "and you have seen Abraham!" "Very truly I tell you," Jesus answered, "before Abraham was born, I am!"

He had finally declared to them who he was, without

a shred of ambiguity. He had used the Divine Identifier, *I am*, based on the name God gave to Moses from the burning bush.

At this, they picked up stones to stone him, but Jesus hid himself, slipping away from the temple grounds.

They had passed judgement with violence. But his time had not yet come, so he eluded them.

What we have seen, in John Chapter 8, was a man, Jesus, in total control of the dialogue, despite the fact that he was faced with 'the metropolitan elite' out to kill him if he were to say the wrong thing. In fact he did condemn himself, but was still able to escape … because his time had not yet come.

But *our* time has come. It is with us now. And so the focus switches to you and me …

What can we learn from this? It compels us to be pro-active in our dealings with the World, for us to set the agenda, rather than defending our position. Jesus spoke with the authority he had from his Father. We have the same authority:

For the grace of God has appeared that offers salvation to all people. It teaches us to say "No" to ungodliness and worldly passions, and to live self-controlled, upright and godly lives in this present age, while we wait for the blessed hope—the appearing of the glory of our great God and Savior, Jesus Christ, who gave himself for us to redeem us from all wickedness and to purify for himself a people that are his very own, eager to do what is good. These, then, are the things you should teach. Encourage and rebuke with all authority. Do not let anyone despise you. (Titus 2:11-15)

This passage should be our mission statement for reaching the World. Let's break it down:

Salvation to all people. The core objective of the Great Commission. If we don't take this important task seriously, then why has God saved us in the first place? *Pass it forward*, that's our goal, whether we accept this or not.

The grace of God teaches us ... this reminds us that what follows is *not from ourselves.*

... to say "no" to ungodliness and worldly passions. What a struggle this has been for Christians in every age. But perhaps there are unprecedented challenges in our day.

... to live self-controlled, upright and godly lives. The proof of the pudding is in the eating. If we reject ungodliness and worldly passions then the evidence will be in the way we live. Our lives must be transparent and uncompromised and a witness to He who lives within us.

While we wait. The 'blessed hope' is our reward but perhaps sometimes we dwell on it a bit too much rather than getting on with the 'job in hand'? Let's dwell on the rainbow now rather than the pot of gold.

Jesus Christ gave himself up for us ... not just so that we can be assured an afterlife!

... to redeem us from all wickedness. To separate us from those who live in "the Kingdom of the World'.

... to purify us. Once separated, we need to be made 'fit for purpose'.

... so that we can be eager to do good. Once made fit, our task lies ahead ... to be good people.

These then are the things you should teach ... i.e. let's concentrate on the following:

... encourage and rebuke with all authority. Here is our God-given authority. The World needs to see us as people with authority, but not as they understand it. This is not the authority of social status, corporate power, celebrity or wealth, but an authority from above.

How is this manifested? That's the 64 million dollar question because there's no easy answer, because we rarely see it exercised. There may have been glimpses of it in earlier times with Martyn Lloyd Jones (even the atheist Joan Bakewell was in awe of him in a TV interview from the 1960s that is available on YouTube), Mary Whitehouse (respected from afar, though the liberal media never acknowledged it at the time) and Mother Teresa. The only person who comes to mind currently is Canon Andrew White, who presents himself as a real person but with a faith that compels him to work in war zones, despite the disability of Multiple Sclerosis.

We need to have this authority, which requires great courage on our part, if we are going to rebuke others. People are happy with the encouragement, but perhaps there is more rebuking to be had if we are going to convince the World that there is a better way. If you haven't already established your authority, then there are possibly going to be some bad outcomes. To explain that, let's consider the final exhortation in the Titus passage.

Do not let anyone despise you.

Christians are largely despised in our current society. Why is that? Is it because we conform to the Christian stereotype that has been constructed by the media? It may be an unfair one, but we have to admit that where there's smoke there's fire. We have to remind ourselves also that in the 'Brave New World' of Cultural Marxism, Christians are Public Enemy #1, irredeemable and out-dated, representatives of an authoritarian – even fascist – hierarchy of dominance and oppression. We are seen as closed, judgemental, unloving, narrow and irrelevant. At times we have probably fitted these negative descriptions quite well. And, after all, didn't Jesus hint that we would be despised?

"If the world hates you, keep in mind that it hated me first. (John 15:18)

We are hated because of Jesus and for what he stands for. It's not that those who live in the world are naturally repelled by him, but that *he who runs amok in the World – the father of lies (and Cultural Marxism) - is poisoning minds against Jesus.*

Perhaps we should make a stand against this and really show who Jesus is, rather than spending our energies judging and criticising those who we call 'sinners', particularly those whose sin is particularly objectionable to us? It was the rulers and leaders and teachers of Jesus' day who despised him, *not the ordinary people.* While he was walking and talking with them, he was greatly loved in his day. So perhaps our goal should be to make Jesus attractive to our generation, to ordinary people rather than those riddled with agendas. If they grow to love us, perhaps they will love our message and *He who is at the centre of the message?*

So, returning to the mission statement for those who wish to communicate with a World gone mad ...

For the grace of God has appeared that offers salvation to all people. It teaches us to say "No" to ungodliness and worldly passions, and to live self-controlled, upright and godly lives in this present age, while we wait for the blessed hope—the appearing of the glory of our great God and Savior, Jesus Christ, who gave himself for us to redeem us from all wickedness and to purify for himself a people that are his very own, eager to do what is good. These, then, are the things you should teach. Encourage and rebuke with all authority. Do not let anyone despise you. (Titus 2:11-15)

In a sentence, ***in order to reach our generation we must first examine ourselves, to turn our back from***

*worldly attractions and embrace godliness - something
that Jesus gives us power to do - so that we can point
people in the right direction, to Jesus himself ... because
they see him in us.*

The times they are a-changin'. It is no longer just what
we say, *it's also what we do and what we are.* Perhaps it
always was!

Loud hailers and amplifiers in public places may
have once worked to drive home a message that
convicted folk of their sin and poor standing before
God, but these days it is not enough.

For a start, because of the changing laws in our
country regarding 'hate speech' and what is 'acceptable'
and 'unacceptable' to say, following a tried and tested
script, loaded with Bible quotes, may land you in a jail
cell if these Bible quotes happen to offend a listener
who, rather than being convicted of sin, feels
empowered to deflect their guilt (often masked as
anger and ire) against the 'giver of the message' with a
quick text, call or email to some 'hateline'.

More importantly, as we have discovered, people
feed their brains in a very different way to even how
things were a couple of years ago. Since Brexit, the
Western World has changed drastically, but most have
not realised it. We are like sheep being coaxed by
wolves masquerading as sheep-dogs into great holding
pens of restrictions, red-tape and controlled behaviour.
We are moving towards a Marxist nightmare of a
'collective' where we are all encouraged or compelled
to think the same way, with a 'false tolerance' of each
other in place of the atmosphere of love and
brotherhood that only Christ can offer – if only *that*
ideal has ever been consistently implemented!

In this 'brave new world' of a post-Christian, post-truth Western culture, we are all flapping around to a certain extent, trying to find an equitable way of getting on with each other. Marxism, communism, capitalism or any other '-ism' is not going to get even close, as history has demonstrated time after time. Only we Christians have the real answer but *are mostly too blind to listen to the words of Scripture* and actually live as we are told to do. That is why it is more important now to not only talk the talk ... but also to *walk the walk*.

Do not let anyone despise you.

How do we do this?

Simple ... we *live the Life*.

Livin' the Life

13

In my previous book, *Livin' the Life*, we learned how to do so by living in … *the Life*. We looked at the need not just to learn about Jesus, but *to model him*. We ended up with three key principles, so often hidden in plain sight, but crucial for a balanced faith walk. These were: **honouring God, reflecting Jesus and engaging with the Holy Spirit**. Here's a bit of an unpacking:

1. Does God get the Glory? We can only answer this if we have a true understanding of God's character and desires. We have to make sure we have a true image of God and not one influenced by the devil's deception, or coloured by our feelings or influenced by the paganism of platonic thinking (from the dualistic teachings of Plato, where the spiritual and the physical are separated). **Are you honouring God?**

2. Are you a good witness to the World? We can only answer this if we have a clear grip on what influences us. Is Jesus at the centre of our life, rather than personal ambition or agenda? Are we truly Hebraic in our lifestyle? Are we people of action or people of words? **Are you reflecting Jesus?**

3. Are you acting in accordance with Holy Scripture, correctly interpreted? We can only answer this if we read God's Word without personal agenda and with proper tools, rather than the 'spiritualising' of the text or the 'rationalising' of Holy Scripture. **Are you engaging with the Holy Spirit?**

Perhaps there are some new ideas here, particularly the need to be *Hebraic?* This may be a confusing term for you. I have already identified Jesus himself as the perfect model for Hebraic thinking when we earlier looked at some episodes in his life and examined how he dealt with those who opposed him. If we define Hebraic thinking as describing the thought processes of the Jews of Biblical times, then obviously Jesus is going to be the perfect example. And the more we reflect him in our thoughts and actions, the more Hebraic we are going to be. It's easier said than done, as I have explained earlier in this book (and in my nine previous books), as we are brought up and educated in the *Greek Mindset*, a totally different way of dealing with life and … if we are brutally honest … a very deficient way of engaging with God.

I would say that it is essential to implement these three principles in all that we do, particularly in our witness to the World. You may *honour God* in your evangelistic efforts, but this needs to be done in a Christ-like attitude and an ear tuned into the promptings of the Holy Spirit. You may show *the servant heart of Jesus* in your dealings with people, but they must be told that you are God's ambassador and are acting in accordance with the direction of the Holy Spirit. You may *operate in the gifts* of tongues and prophecy, but do you glorify God in acknowledging Him as the true source and does Jesus shine out through you as you minister to others?

We are all more Greek than we realise. We have history and the processes of society to thank for this. There are people I know who wear the label 'Christian' with great pride, who are pillars of the local church, always the first to pray in public, speak to the stranger and speak of Jesus fearlessly. Yet ... when it comes to conduct and dealings with people in their private life, it's a totally different picture. The external mask does not truly reflect the internal motivations. It's not Jesus shining through, it's a safe replica. There is an absence of that much-maligned Christian term, *holiness*. We would do well to truly dwell on this verse:

And we all, who with unveiled faces contemplate the Lord's glory, are being transformed into his image with ever-increasing glory, which comes from the Lord, who is the Spirit. (2 Corinthians 3:18)

This is holiness, living a life that is different from all around, so much so that people are inclined to think, *hey there's something different going on here.* I am reminded of an editorial by David Andrew in an issue of Sword magazine, in the Summer of 2017.

There is a God-given, God-ordained uniqueness that separates Church from society, Christian from non-Christian. If society blurs the distinctions between black and white, truth and falsehood, right and wrong, Jesus and Muhammad, what 'difference' can be accomplished by politically correct Christians who simply blend in – whose lives never challenge the world's twisted versions of truth and reality? The issue is UNIQUENESS.

Uniqueness, holiness, separation. It's all connected. We are called to be different as well as making a difference. We are not called to 'blend-in' to 'add a flavour of Christianity into the mix', as some Christians seem to be doing. David Andrew argues that there must be a discernible gap between Christians and the World, between the Kingdom of God and the Kingdom of the World. He continues:

But, glorious as is our hope, it reveals for now and for our time, why the gap between the true Church and the world can never be closed. It's easily understood when we realise that the gap is Jesus. You can blend the Bride only if you can blend the Groom. A Jesus made to suit the world's tastes would never have been crucified; He would have been celebrated. When He died, He would have stayed dead like every other sinner in history. In Lewis' famous description, "death itself works backwards" only for a spotless sacrifice. As we can see, Satan uses countless strategies to try to close the gap. He loves it when Christians unquestioningly accept the world's fashionable views on sexuality, Israel and the Jews, world religions, abortion, marriage and parenthood etc. He has even more fun when Christians are so ignorant of the Bible that they don't even realise they have an on-going (unwinnable) argument with God.

And the key to all of this is true Hebraic living. Let's recap before we move on.

1. The starting place for understanding Hebraic thinking and living is to look at the example of Jesus himself, the *ultimate Hebrew of Hebrews*. He was thoroughly acquainted with the Hebrew Scriptures and often used this knowledge to thwart his accusers, such as with those accusing the woman caught in adultery. He also validated his own teachings and claims about himself with signs and wonders, such as in the healing of the paralysed man. He had a perfect connection with the Spirit and so was never lost for the right words to use in each occasion. Sometimes he was sparing with these, allowing for maximum impact, such as at his trial in the Sanhedrin, when he finally revealed to them clearly his divine authority and mission. At other times he engaged with his detractors in lengthy dialogues, answering their questions and posing some of his own. Of course we are not Jesus, but we do act in his

authority, so he provides us with *the* model to use when communicating with others.

2. A workable mission statement to use is provided in the words of Titus 2:11-15, paraphrased as: *in order to reach our generation we must first examine ourselves, to turn our back from worldly attractions and embrace godliness - something that Jesus gives us power to do - so that we can point people in the right direction, to Jesus himself ... because they see him in us.* So, when we look at Jesus as our model, this is not an academic exercise, but a true intention of **becoming a collection of 'little Jesuses'.**

3. Now is where the rubber hits the road. How do we become 'little Jesuses'? A good place to start is to be mindful of the three principles; honouring God, reflecting Jesus and engaging with the Holy Spirit. Let's face it, this is all pretty obvious, but sometimes our Christian lives have lost simplicity and direction, as we have allowed our Greek impulses to skew our priorities away from the basic requirements. When this happens, our witness to the World suffers and the gap between us and the World diminishes possibly to the extent that there is *really no difference between us and the non-believer.*

There is more to being Hebraic that can help us in maintaining a significant gap. Here are a few ideas from my book, *To Life*, that should help:

From looking at the Golden Rule, the Sermon on the Mount and the Book of James the core of Hebraic living is that; Faith in God underpins our wisdom, which compels us to perform our deeds. This is Hebrew thinking, the Hebraic mindset. The key to the Hebraic mindset is faith in God and the result of the Hebraic mindset is the performing of deeds. Faith and works, they are at the heart of our Christian faith, our Hebraic Christian faith.

The significant factor when performing our deeds is

that they are in accordance with Godly wisdom, as described in James 3:17

"But the wisdom that comes from heaven is first of all pure; then peace-loving, considerate, submissive, full of mercy and good fruit, impartial and sincere."

This is in contrast to the 'wisdom' characterised by the world, the flesh and the devil:

But if you harbour bitter envy and selfish ambition in your hearts, do not boast about it or deny the truth. Such "wisdom" does not come down from heaven but is earthly, unspiritual, of the devil. For where you have envy and selfish ambition, there you find disorder and every evil practice. (James 3:14-16)

So, good deeds, initiated by our faith in God and undergirded by good wisdom. Simple really. Here are some examples of good wisdom, in the way of contrasts between Hebraic and Greek thinking.

- The Greek mind says that man is at the centre of life; the Hebraic mind says that God is at the centre of life.

- The Greek mind says that the things of God must be deduced from our logical minds; the Hebraic mind says that the things of God can only be understood by faith and revelation.

- The Greek mind says that we should strive for knowledge about God; the Hebraic mind says that we should know God.

These are just words and concepts. We need to let them really sink in and soak us in their truths. It may take time, but it will be worth it. It really is *thinking differently*. But to really think differently we are now *really* going to stretch you.

Form and function. Here is an extract from *Hebraic Church* to get you started:

These days we have lost the sense of this, even us Christians. With our Greek mindsets we judge by appearance, not function. That's an ugly so-and-so, *we might exclaim at a Canaanite Baal figurine, judging its lack of physical beauty but ignoring the fact that this so-and-so was worshipped as god even by some who should have known better.* Ahab, yes it's you we're talking about here!

We may worship a celebrity (the word is from the Latin word for 'honoured one') because of her beauty, or a sportsman because of his ball skills, or a pop star because of his fine voice. This is all about the form, *the physical attributes of the 'object of adoration'. The* function *addresses the thoughts and feelings provoked in our spirits by the celebrity, sportsman or pop star. We throw resources at them (merchandising) and devote time to them (thinking about, watching or listening). They become an alternative to He with Whom we should be spending time and resources. Moderation is the watchword here, as the last thing we want is to be distracted away from our destiny as disciples of God.*

There is another way of looking at this. We are a culture totally obsessed with form, *in our reverence for and even worship of, physical beauty. But those of us of a more discerning nature would look at* inner beauty, *the character, the personality, the function of that person, in the way that they interact with those around them. We know far more about the function than the form of most Bible characters. We know little about physical characteristics. The rare exception being a description of King David.*

He was ruddy, with a fine appearance and handsome features. (1 Samuel 16:12)

That's about it. That could be describing me (in your

dreams, mate!) *We may not be able to paint a portrait from this sketchy description, but we could write essays about his character, his exploits, his good points and bad points. One just needs to read the Psalms that David authored, but here's an insight into his great and practical faith: his decision to take on Goliath:*

"Your servant has killed both the lion and the bear; this uncircumcised Philistine will be like one of them, because he has defied the armies of the living God. The LORD who delivered me from the paw of the lion and the paw of the bear will deliver me from the hand of this Philistine." (1 Samuel 17:36-37)

So the function *of King David was his faith and trust, as well as his devotion, his poetry, recklessness, brutality ... You can see where I'm going here, because the Bible paints very thorough portraits of the character of its characters, warts and all. This is because we can learn much by studying their actions just as we learn little from studying their physical appearance or circumstance.*

So we have met *form and function.* Believe me, *they are the key to thinking Hebraically.* And, because we are not trained to consider things in this way, **they are also the key to thinking differently.**

At the time of writing the above, a couple of years ago, I sensed that they were the key to thinking Hebraically, but I hadn't really thought this through thoroughly. Since then I have realised that this simple concept is far more important than I had ever thought, in fact I would go as far as to say that **it is at the very core of the Gospel message.** God's plan is to create a family of people who will ultimately live with Him in eternity. Our suitability for this privilege is our willingness to be a people defined by our function, not our form, people with actions and deeds, rather than people sitting on their hands and 'waiting for heaven'.

But it's not just about us, it's about the World we have created. Here's a defining statement that puts this into perspective:

We have created forms out of much that God designed as functions.

Here are some examples that should make you think.

Worship is a function that pours out of the desire within our heart to acknowledge the One Who has Created us and redeemed us.

Exalt the LORD our God and worship at his footstool; he is holy. (Psalm 99:5)

It is an action, a 'doing', a verb. Our current Christian culture has often turned it into an object, a noun, even a commodity. When we speak of a 'time of worship' we often stress the time element, wedged between other time elements, during which we will engage in acts of worship. In the Western Church this is often a fixed time, comprised of a schedule of pre-selected songs, in contrast to, say, the African church, when it is usually more free-flowing and open-ended. The concept of worship, the desire within the heart to express thanksgiving and praise to God, is meant to be spontaneous, untamed even. It has been used to create a genre of nouns; worship leaders, worship music, praise & worship. It is even monetised. Yes this may seem like a very cynical deconstruction, particularly to those who are involved in 'worship', but sometimes we need to strip down to the core motivations of what we do, always remembering Divine origins and purposes.

How could things be different in our Church life if

worship was acknowledged *more as a function than a form?* Perhaps it would be freed up from 'orders of service', as a spontaneous act that flows naturally from what God is doing with you as an individual and a congregation. I have been to many African services where this happens and, to the Western eye, it may seem messy and disorganised and no respecter of time (don't they have a concept of set lunchtimes?!) but I would describe this as Hebraic and perhaps more in keeping with how the early Church behaved. Perhaps it would also free us up individually, to be *people* (noun) *of worship* (verb) or people who worship.

Wearing a linen ephod, David was dancing before the LORD with all his might, while he and all Israel were bringing up the ark of the LORD with shouts and the sound of trumpets. (2 Samuel 6:14-15)

This may be too much for some. But surely love of God should always trump fear of man? Perhaps someone should have mentioned this to David's wife?

As the ark of the LORD was entering the City of David, Michal daughter of Saul watched from a window. And when she saw King David leaping and dancing before the LORD, she despised him in her heart. (Verse 16)

I often wish I were more spontaneous, but there's a constant fight against British reserve. In my travels I often meet *people who worship*, folk who exude a love of God and *don't care who witnesses it*. Surely this must be the best form of evangelism, as it marks us out as different, even if this difference is a cultural anomaly. All we need to do is break through our personal embarrassment threshold and allow our inner selves to shine through to the outside. Easier said than done!

Prayer is another activity that suffers in the same

way. The fact that it doesn't come as naturally to some of us is perhaps, unconsciously, that it has become a form rather than a function. We create an activity known as a *prayer meeting*, usually one of the lowest attended meetings in the church diary. Have you ever wondered why? Could it be because, for some, prayer is a private activity (just between me and my Creator) and why traipse outdoors to meet with others to do what can be adequately done as a solo exercise? Yet, there is power in communal prayer:

"Again, truly I tell you that if two of you on earth agree about anything they ask for, it will be done for them by my Father in heaven. For where two or three gather in my name, there am I with them." (Matthew 18:19-20)

This is an awesome statement when read as if it encountered for the first time. This guarantees that Jesus will turn up at a prayer meeting even if others don't. Imagine if we advertise our meetings thusways; *come to our prayer meeting, Jesus has promised to be there, how about you?*

Meetings can be the bane of our lives in our culture. That's just my view, as my experience has always been that more is achieved by informal endeavours rather than locking a group of people together for hours on end and expecting a favourable outcome. You, of course, may be more favourably disposed ...

Meetings are the ultimate *form*, even though, in many cases, they are necessary to get things done, where there is true synergy between participants. In their worst manifestation they are like malign holding pens, brought into being by bureaucratic meddling and serve only to eat away at the hours of a working day or to rubberstamp decisions already made. If there is any *function* attached to such proceedings it is simply to sap life and hope out of the participants.

Let's not forget who we are, *children of the King*. Let's meet together by all means, as long as it is to bless each other and our Creator. A prayer meeting really needs to be such an event. We need to create a function out of this form, by reminding everyone of the *function* that we have come to perform and the promises Jesus made to us regarding his star billing!

Also … we need to be *people who pray*. We need to live as if praying is as natural to us as eating and breathing, a true function of the human spirit. Again, I am constantly meeting people who seem to be in continuous dialogue with God (though, in reality, it tends to veer towards monologue), involving Him in all aspects of their lives. This, of course, is truly Hebraic and Jesus himself provides the best model for this attitude:

Then Jesus told his disciples a parable to show them that they should always pray and not give up. (Luke 18:1)

Paul, of course, told us to *pray without ceasing.* (1 Thessalonians 5:17)

One new acquaintance of mine impressed me on a particularly hazardous car journey up a steep hill in Wales by praying continuously while driving up the single track road, so that no car would be encountered in the opposite direction! This he did in such a natural manner, interspersing his conversation with his passengers with his Divine requests. I'm sure God smiles when we include Him in our everyday lives, an incredibly important Person in our lives who just happens to be invisible.

If you want to get angry and dismayed as to how low

some prominent Christians have stooped, just give a listen to some of the 'faith' preachers on Christian TV. Their concept of **faith** comes from nowhere apart from their own faithlessness and greed. The most common Biblical definition is Hebrews 11:1. This is the one that the 'faith' preachers use to justify their errant behaviour and it is the King James version that they use to push their point home. Here is the King James translation of that verse:

Now faith is the substance of things hoped for, the evidence of things not seen.

There is one key word here, around which their empires hang, the single word that has provided them with Lear Jets, multi-million dollar ministries and a vast army of duped followers. The word is *substance*.

Here is how Kenneth Copeland, one of the 'fathers' of the prosperity and faith teachers, understands this word in how he defines 'faith'.

"Faith is a spiritual force ... It is substance. Faith has the ability to effect natural substance."

This definition is faulty and it comes from the pagan philosophy of Aristotle, who sees substance as a form, an object made of matter. Taking this definition, Copeland and his 'gang of clones' view *faith* as a form, a tangible object or force that can be measured and quantified and used as a key to break open the financial storehouses of heaven and bring untold riches.

The Greek word translated as 'substance' in the KJV is *hypostasis* and is better translated as a 'channel of trust' between man and God, very much a function, rather than a form. Here are some other translations of this verse.

Now faith is confidence in what we hope for and assurance

about what we do not see. (NIV)

Trusting is being confident of what we hope for, convinced about things we do not see. (Complete Jewish Bible)

Faith makes us sure of what we hope for and gives us proof of what we cannot see. (Contemporary English Version)

So, *faith* is a doing word, a verb, rather than a noun. Having faith is an activity we exercise tied up in our trust in God, rather than a commodity to be cashed in. Hopefully you are beginning to see how our culture (including our Christian culture) has surrounded us with a Greek-inspired universe of *forms,* yet God would prefer us to think Hebraically (Biblically) and rather consider us as a community of *functions.*

Shouldn't Christians be known by what we *do* (function), rather than what we *are* (form), because, after all, isn't that we were put on Earth for?

For we are God's handiwork, created in Christ Jesus to do good works, which God prepared in advance for us to do. (Ephesians 2:10)

Are we 'pastors' or do we pastor? Are we 'evangelists' or do we evangelise? Are we teachers/preachers/prophets etc.? The point is that there can be a world of difference between the 'office' and the function and many people exercise their God-given functions without the luxury of a prestigious title. Understanding this can open up a whole new Universe for us, particularly when we consider that our function **must** be our God-given function, *rather than something we play at because it makes us feel good or important.*

Take the thorny and misunderstood subject of *healing.* We so often see it as a form, with our healing services or our assertions of 'grab your healing' or 'believe you are healed'. These all put the onus on us rather than God Himself, the Healer. It is not an exact science, it's not even a science, it is an outworking of God's grace to an individual, in His own timing and for His own Glory. It's not about us, it's all about Him. He heals who He heals, just as He chooses who He chooses. *"Just as it is written: "Jacob I loved, but Esau I hated."* (Romans 9:13). Rather than viewing healing as a form that can be earned/acquired by accruing sufficient 'faith brownie points' or (God forbid!) paying enough to certain 'healing evangelists', it is a Divine function that flows in the reverse direction, from God to man, in order to fulfil His purposes. This is not to say that we shouldn't pray for healing, as God may have His purposes, but He is still moved by our petitions – there is absolutely no doubt about that!

"But God has surely listened and has heard my prayer." (Psalm 66:19)

"But Moses sought the favor of the LORD his God … Turn from your fierce anger; relent and do not bring disaster on your people. … Then the LORD relented and did not bring on his people the disaster he had threatened." (Exodus 32:11-14)

Function and form are actually a part of our daily lives. On one level we ought to consider people for what they do, rather than how they look. On another level, a personal incident comes to mind. I am one of those people who wears a FitBit tracker, endeavouring to walk 10,000 steps daily. One day, after a two mile hike, I realised I had forgotten to slip it on my wrist that morning. At the end of that day, despite walking four miles, I felt inadequate and under-exercised, not that I hadn't put in the work (the function) but rather that I had failed to record it (the form)!

The whole essence of function rather than form and of the Hebraic mindset in general is to continually remind ourselves that *God is in control, not us* and that we are on this Earth as His vessels of grace, in order to do our part in fulfilling His purposes.

His intent was that now, through the church, the manifold wisdom of God should be made known to the rulers and authorities in the heavenly realms, according to his eternal purpose that he accomplished in Christ Jesus our Lord. (Ephesians 3:10-11)

Let's be reminded of this incredibly difficult passage written by Paul to the church in Galatia:

"For through the law I died to the law so that I might live for God. I have been crucified with Christ and I no longer live, but Christ lives in me. The life I now live in the body, I live by faith in the Son of God, who loved me and gave himself for me. I do not set aside the grace of God, for if righteousness could be gained through the law, Christ died for nothing!" (Galatians 2:19-21)

What Paul is saying is that although the World sees him as a form – a middle aged stroppy Jew – his true desire is to act as God's *function*, with God living in him through his faith in the risen Christ.

With that in mind, let's move on ...

The Heart of the Problem

14

The concept of form and function is our best weapon in dealing with the problem of Cultural Marxism. It's the KISS principle in action (Keep it Simple, Stupid!) and it helps to expose what's really at the heart of the problem.

Let's consider one of the hottest topics in our culture today, that of *gender fluidity*. To gain an understanding of this confusing situation, we will work our way towards it, starting with basic biology. I have to be honest, it was extremely difficult to get basic material on the traditional view, as the web has been hijacked by the newer manifestations of sexual and gender identity. It's a perfect example of postmodern murkiness, reminiscent of the rabbis' meanderings in the Talmud; you start off with a basic given truth and then you totally obscure it with commentary, research and opinion. Stripping this away in the best way that I could, I ended up with this ...

So God created mankind in his own image, in the image of God he created them; male and female he created them. (Genesis 1:27)

So there is male and there is female in the original creation. Of course, as a result of The Fall and man's sin, physical diseases and aberrations can affect the DNA and produce physical conditions such as *hermaphroditism*, where the body exhibits both male and female sexual parts and mental conditions such as *gender dysphoria*, where a mind may be uncomfortable with the assigned biological sex. Recent statistics indicate that gender dysphoria affects around 1 in 10,000 people (0.01% of the population) and hermaphroditism affects about 1 in 2,000 people (0.05% of the population).

So, given the rarity of these conditions, why is the transgender agenda so influential in society? In 2015 the Office for National Statistics had 1.7% of the UK population as lesbian, gay or bisexual, with 0.4% as transsexual. Again, very small numbers, though you wouldn't have expected that considering the cultural impact on our society. In Germany a top court has ruled that birth certificates should now have the option of a third sex (i.e. anything other than male or female). Such a major development to cater for such a miniscule proportion of society? Is this an over-reaction to a (perhaps) non-existent 'problem'? Or has our World really gone mad?

The heart of the problem is not these statistics, nor is it the people who constitute these statistics, but rather the people who have created an *agenda* out of the purported issue. These people are working through the ideas of Cultural Marxism and have created a 'victim group' out of those in the LGBTIQ+ community and, by doing so, have transformed these communities from self-help groups to a *celebration* of diversity. This, then, is promoted as a thoroughly 'good thing' because it emphasises the division between the oppressors (the straight 'binary' community, constituting 97.9% of society) and the oppressed (those who are encouraged to join the LGBTIQ+ community as a matter of choice).

An example of this is demonstrated in a 2017 BBC drama, set in a registry office. In a single episode we saw a Jewish same-sex marriage, with a full turnout of stock Jewish characters, all beaming their approval. We also had someone undergoing a 'transformation' from man to woman, with approval from all apart from a single character. This character is depicted as cunning and sour-faced and is, as expected, a Christian stereotype. A key plot strand is the conflict between this character and the 'heroine', who is fully accepting of the LGBTIQ+ agenda. It turns out that the 'baddie' has secretly refused to go on the list of staff agreeing to conduct same-sex marriages and the 'heroine' is using this discovery as leverage in the conflict between the two. In other words, we are drawn into the atmosphere of acceptance of the LGBTIQ+ agenda, because of the way the characters are drawn by the scriptwriter. It's all subtle, but it is all indoctrination. In a few years' time most people will see this whole thing as a non-issue in the 'progressive' (Marxist) society that we are becoming.

Laying aside propaganda, the fact is that, apart from those suffering from a physical or mental condition, joining the LGBTIQ+ community really is a *matter of choice*. A choice has been made by the individual to re-classify their biological sex by emphasising their gender *identity*. This is the key word, *identity*.

'Identity' is at the heart of Critical Theory, the mechanism that drives Cultural Marxism. It is a perfect example of a form. It is telling the World, *my gender identity is the most important part of me, in fact, now that our culture is so progressive, I openly celebrate it.* The corollary to this is that anyone who is obstructive to this 'human right', for instance refusing to bake a cake declaring this 'celebration', is an oppressor and is to be reported to the authorities. Surely there's a big difference between acceptance and celebration? We can accept a personal choice someone has made, but we shouldn't be forced to celebrate this fact in the same way that I don't ask non-believers to celebrate my decision to follow Jesus as my Lord and Saviour (though the angels are pretty pleased by this – Luke 15:10).

Concentrating on *form* is looking inwards and placing yourself at the centre of the Universe. It is a natural outworking of the Kingdom of the World, as much a feature of postmodernism as it was for secular humanism that preceded this. Christians, instead, should be concentrating on *function*.

Therefore, my dear friends, as you have always obeyed—not only in my presence, but now much more in my absence—continue to work out your salvation with fear and trembling, for it is God who works in you to will and to act in order to fulfill his good purpose. (Philippians 2:12-13)

For Christians, though, we have a situation where form and function come together ... gloriously. And it is all a question of identity, *our identity in Jesus.*

And we all, who with unveiled faces contemplate the Lord's glory, are being transformed into his image with ever-increasing glory, which comes from the Lord, who is the Spirit. (2 Corinthians 3:18)

Our *function* is to strive to imitate the form of Jesus, as we have seen in earlier Chapters. It should always be *not me, but Christ who lives in me* (Galatians 2:20). Our *function* is to allow Christ to live in us and lead us into the work that he has for us.

For we are God's handiwork, created in Christ Jesus to do good works, which God prepared in advance for us to do. (Ephesians 2:10)

Our identity should therefore be precious to us, but not our past identity, defined by race, culture or family, but our future identity, when we will be presented to Jesus ... *as a radiant church, without stain or wrinkle or any other blemish, but holy and blameless.* (Ephesians 5:27)

The 'enemy', through his chosen tool of Cultural Marxism, has taken this concept of *identity* and twisted and corrupted it. He has used this to pigeon-hole people into controllable groups, by emphasising their form and dismissing their function. It compels people to believe they are defined by their form, whether it is a matter of race, colour or gender inclination, to an extent that they lose any freedom they may have had to express themselves as individuals. Identity has become a bondage rather than something that can benefit people - the ultimate goal of undermining the traditional structures of society and bringing in the extensive State control that Cultural Marxists crave.

The strategy is the same for all of the other artificial 'victim groups' they have created. The 1960s saw the growth of the Civil Rights movement in the USA, in order to improve the status of black people who had been discriminated against for ages. The Civil Rights Act in 1964 outlawed segregation in schools, public places and jobs, followed by the Voting Rights Act and the Fair Housing Act. It was all very worthy and it gave us Marin Luther King Jr. as a highly respected icon of the movement. This is true social justice in action.

Now we have a new movement, *Black Lives Matter* (BLM), formed in 2013 by three female activists in the USA. It campaigns against racism against black people but seems to only represent a minority of the black community, arguably the more radical and edgy elements. Most black people in the West who have integrated into society have concentrated on careers and calling and *not* identity. The thinking is that, as long as their identity is not creating issues for them, then they would rather dwell on issues of function and purpose. BLM, along with similar groups such as *Antifa* ('anti-fascists' who ironically dress up as fascists and behave like storm-troopers) and *Stop the War Coalition* exist solely to protest and divide and are willing foot soldiers for Cultural Marxism.

You can look and look but, although you will find groups representing such 'victims' as Muslims, LGBTIQ+, Palestinians, the environment, racial minorities and pacifists, you will not find any group defending arguably the most victimised groups in the world today; Christians (particularly in Muslim countries) and, particularly, Jews. Jewish people may have invented and implemented Cultural Marxism, but they are certainly not benefitting from it as a community. Think about *Islamophobia*. It's an artificial construct in order to push a particular narrative and agenda. A phobia is an irrational fear, yet fear of Muslim-inspired terrorism is totally rational, particularly as so many of the protagonists are characterised by the statement, *but they seemed like an ordinary quiet family.* There is no Buddhistphobia, Hinduphobia, Christian-ophobia or Jewphobia, by the way.

If there's any evidence as to the ultimate intentions of this process, then there it is. For Cultural Marxists, the only acceptable narratives for Jews and Christians is either to see them as eternal aggressors (Christians) or arch manipulators (Jews).

At the time of writing the 'victim' culture is running amok, with Hollywood and Parliament the current battlefields. For years people jokingly referred to the producer's 'casting couch', which obviously had a grounding in reality. Now the odious Harvey Weinstein episode has exploded with seemingly every male (heterosexual and homosexual) associated with the film industry who had touched someone else inappropriately twenty years ago being exposed, with contracts torn up, awards withdrawn and actors airbrushed out of films. Considering that these shenanigans had been known about for years, why is there now such a conveyor belt of 'victims'? The serious stories, of course, need to be told and dealt with to show what a disgusting place Hollywood was and still is, but one wonders how some may be cashing in empty cheques, unwilling to admit the consensual nature of the 'dastardly deed' as a passport to fame. Surely, like it or not, that's how Hollywood works.

There's a similar story with our politicians, with many chickens coming home to roost. Major figures are being forced to resign on such flimsy pretexts of an 'accidental hand on the knee fifteen years ago' and, although we have always known that our elected representatives have not always been paragons of virtue, we are seeing a fresh explosion of the 'victim' culture that is at the heart of Cultural Marxism.

Everyone seems to be offended about something and our lawyers have never had things so good! We really are a generation of 'snowflakes', particularly if we remember the current atmosphere in our universities, with their 'safe spaces' and lists of do's and don'ts, the *micro-aggressions*.

God forbid if there was ever a serious war! Those grandparents and great-grandparents who have lived through the 1930s and 40s must despair of our rising generation. We have been softened up, our individualism has been clawed away from us as we continue in our lives of 'personal entitlement' and 'human rights', all sanctioned by the Marxist forces that surround us.

The cat is out of the bag. Now the focus returns to us ...

Equipping ourselves

15

Earlier Chapters have given us a better idea of what is involved in living Hebraically, the best way of dealing with Cultural Marxism and its growing restrictions on Christians. We therefore have the basic building blocks, the alphabet, but need to now construct a model for ... communicating with a World gone mad.

This has to be eminently useable and practical as we ought to be beyond the Greek model of 'head knowledge' and into this scary new realm of finding the best way to communicate our faith not only to those who don't know Jesus but also, sadly, to some who think they do know him!

It's time for another recap to remind ourselves of the building blocks.

1. We remind ourselves through re-reading the Gospels, of how Jesus communicated, as he must be our model for true Hebraic thinking and acting. The keys are his thorough knowledge of Scripture, his seamless connection to his Father through prayer and the wisdom that flowed accordingly.

2. We heed the words of Titus 2:11-15, paraphrased as: *in order to reach our generation we must first examine ourselves, to turn our back from worldly attractions and embrace godliness - something that Jesus gives us power to do - so that we can point people in the right direction, to Jesus himself ... because they see him in us.*

3. We are mindful of the three principles; honouring God, reflecting Jesus and engaging with the Holy Spirit.

4. We follow the Godly wisdom as described in James 3:17 *"But the wisdom that comes from heaven is first of all pure; then peace-loving, considerate, submissive, full of mercy and good fruit, impartial and sincere."*

5. We always consider God's perspective rather than our own and learn to differentiate between form and function, the former being the Greek way of ordering the Universe, but the latter being God's Hebraic way that we should view the World.

6. We seek to discover our true *function* within the Body of Christ, in accordance with God's will for our lives. *For we are God's handiwork, created in Christ Jesus to do good works, which God prepared in advance for us to do.* (Ephesians 2:10)

These are our building blocks. Let's contrast them with the building blocks by which the World operates.

1. The World presents no standard working model for human behaviour. There is no single accepted example to follow, so we are free to choose one that works for us, be it a family member, a friend or a celebrity. We have no way of judging how good a choice this is as we live in a World where morality and truth is relative.

2. The basic driving force in the World is self-preservation, which is why we tend to vote for politicians who can best benefit ourselves and our families in the short-term, rather than the long-term benefits for the country. Most people have no desire other than the pursuit of personal pleasure and hopefully to die peacefully in their sleep at a ripe old age.

3. If people do have principles that they live by they would usually be to stay out of trouble and live a quiet life. Morality tends to be results-driven, in that most people are untroubled by absolute morality or ethics and, if presented with a personally advantageous yet ethically dubious situation that has no negative come-backs, they would follow it with an untroubled conscience. This is why abortion statistics are so high and how many are untroubled by such issues as voluntary euthanasia.

4. Although there are notable exceptions, in terms of 'wisdom' most non-believers follow the darker side of James 3:14-16. *But if you harbour bitter envy and selfish ambition in your hearts, do not boast about it or deny the truth. Such "wisdom" does not come down from heaven but is earthly, unspiritual, of the devil. For where you have envy and selfish ambition, there you find disorder and every evil practice.*

5. The World follows man's ways not God's and, with the accent on materialism and individualism, is mostly more interested in forms than function, in the pursuit of money, power, physical beauty, sexual gratification and fame, rather than a sense of contributing to the common good.

6. Most people in the World rarely have a sense of purpose (or function) beyond selfish ambitions.

This may appear to be a bit black and white and there are obviously exceptions to the general rule, with some truly altruistic non-believing individuals. One only has to look at an earlier generation to see how many freely gave of their lives in wars out of love of country, as well as the selfless band of charity and relief workers who give of their time to help others. Sadly these are exceptions and many may actually be on a journey that they are currently unaware of, but which will be revealed to them one day. In this book we are looking at the big picture, the zeitgeist, the majority World views. Most people you come in contact with will be living according to the rules just listed above.

If we are truly in God's Kingdom then we need to be aware of the 'building blocks' we are using as we witness for Jesus in our present-day World. **And we need to make sure we stick with them.** Although our evangelism has a core purpose of seeing people convicted of their sins and their need for a Saviour, to ensure a path to heaven, we need to work with a dual purpose. Because their salvation is all very well, but they also need to find their God-ordained purpose in this life, to fulfil their destiny as a New Creation.

So, following on from the six rules above, we need to see them:

- Accepting Jesus as the model for their new life.

- Demonstrating Jesus living inside them.

- Not just reflecting Jesus, but honouring God and engaging with the Holy Spirit.

- Showing Godly wisdom in their decision making.

- Seeking to honour others and working for the benefit of others.

- Discovering what their role is in God's Kingdom.

And for this to happen, they need to see these things … *in us.* Accordingly, there may be a need to rethink the way we do our evangelism. Here's what I said in *Livin' the Life*:

When I look at us Christians and the way we are taught to do our evangelism, I was first drawn to a simplification, perhaps even a caricature of the process. And it spoke volumes to me. It seems that the primary goal *of the Christianity that we are propagating is eternal life for the individual. The* means *that this is achieved is a 'one-time' recital of the 'sinner's prayer', such as the one here:*

Dear Lord Jesus, I know that I am a sinner, and I ask for Your forgiveness. I believe You died for my sins and rose from the dead. I turn from my sins and invite You to come into my heart and life. I want to trust and follow You as my Lord and Saviour. In Your Name. Amen.

This could be misunderstood as a 'magic' formula or incantation, as if the process of repeating these words is sufficient to blaze a trail into the halls of eternal life. If it is, then this is Christianity-lite, commitment-free, Hope-zero; seeds of the Great Omission (rather than the Great Commission), something has been removed, a 'conversion' without commitment, a transaction without consequence.

Of course, the heart may have already been primed for this life-changing prayer. This may be a culmination of Holy Spirit nudges over a period of time, with the deal finally sealed and the heavenly choir truly activated. Or ... here is a telling quote by Paul Washer (truthsource.net):

"In modern day evangelism, this precious doctrine [of regeneration] has been reduced to nothing more than a human decision to raise one's hand, walk an aisle, or pray a 'sinner's prayer.' As a result, the majority of Americans believe that they've been 'born again' even though their thoughts, words, and deeds are a continual contradiction to the nature and will of God."

Does this mean that many in the 'Church' may not even be saved? What a horrible thought. This is serious business and we need to remind ourselves what ought to be the focus of our evangelism. Nothing less than to produce Christians of the ilk of the Acts 2 church, where the primary goal or objective is to reflect Jesus. *The means by which this is accomplished is* engagement with the Holy Spirit *and the sign that this has happened is that our lives become God-centred, that we* honour *God above all. Our three basic principles in action!*

Surely in our current climate a more holistic approach is needed. Why should I say that? Well, let's first consider a few recent incidents in the UK. These are taken from the records of *Christian Concern*, based on their reports at *http://www.christianconcern.com/cases*

• Two street preachers were convicted in February 2017 of a 'religiously aggravated' public order offence. They had been publicly discussing the differences between Christianity and Islam. Most tellingly, the prosecutor had argued, "*to say to someone that Jesus is the only God is not a matter of truth. To the extent that they are saying that the only way to God is through Jesus, that cannot be a truth.*" They were eventually acquitted.

• Another street preacher had been arrested in March 2017 for causing harassment, alarm and distress to two men in a homosexual relationship. He had quoted from Luke 13:1-5 and Matthew 15:19. He was eventually aquitted.

• A Christian nurse was fired by the NHS for talking to patients about her faith and offering to pray for them. She was dismissed in August 2016 for 'gross misconduct'.

• A Christian magistrate was disciplined by a Cabinet minister and England's highest judge for saying that a child's best interests lie in being raised by a mother and father (rather than a same-sex couple).

• A gardener at a prison was forced to resign after a

complaint was made concerning Bible verses he quoted as a volunteer in a chapel service. He told the hearing in November 2014, *"As I led the service, I spoke about the wonder of God's love and the forgiveness that comes through Jesus to those who recognise their sin and repent. I said that I am the worst sinner I know."* The prosecution asserted that he was preaching forgiveness *in an "insensitive" way which "failed to have regard for the special nature of the congregation in the prison".*

• A Christian student was removed from his university social work course after he made comments on his personal Facebook page in support of Biblical teaching on marriage and sexual ethics. He was told that, by posting his comments, he *"may have caused offence to some individuals" and had "transgressed boundaries which are not deemed appropriate for someone entering the Social Work profession."*

These examples (and there are plenty more if you visit the Christian Concern website) prove the sad but unavoidable truth that *we are no longer a Christian country.* The insidious effect of Cultural Marxism on our society has painted us as the new counter-culture, the outsiders who don't fit in with 'progressive' society or the eternal 'aggressors' in the far-left narrative that drives everything in the public arena these days.

Whether we are pro-actively evangelising in public places or in our workplace or simply responding to questions about our faith, or even living out our faith the best that we can, we are the outsiders looking in. We are in the best of company – **that is how the early Church operated.**

You, however, know all about my teaching, my way of life, my purpose, faith, patience, love, endurance, persecutions, sufferings—what kinds of things happened to me in Antioch, Iconium and Lystra, the persecutions I endured. Yet the Lord rescued me from all of them. In fact, everyone who wants to live a godly life in Christ Jesus will be persecuted, while evildoers and impostors will go from bad to worse, deceiving and being deceived. (2 Timothy 3:10-13)

Perhaps we have had it too good for too long. Perhaps we have become flaccid, inward-looking, compromised and complacent. *Perhaps we are now in a better place than we ever realised!*

Dear friends, do not be surprised at the fiery ordeal that has come on you to test you, as though something strange were happening to you. But rejoice inasmuch as you participate in the sufferings of Christ, so that you may be overjoyed when his glory is revealed. If you are insulted because of the name of Christ, you are blessed, for the Spirit of glory and of God rests on you. (1 Peter 4:12-14)

"Blessed are those who are persecuted for righteousness' sake, for theirs is the kingdom of heaven." (Matthew 5:10)

This is an interesting situation, perhaps unique. Earlier societies, such as the Roman era or Tudor times, when Christians were persecuted, didn't have a network of instant communication and information flow as we have today with social media and the web. In earlier times, persecution was at the hands of those in absolute power, whether emperors, kings or the established Church. We see the same in modern times in developing countries, where anti-Christian persecution is instigated by the imams and mullahs and carried out by those under their control.

By contrast, in the West today, persecution is far more subtle. You don't necessarily need to be visible to your persecutors, as a church-goer or a participant at a pro-Christian rally. All you might need to do is type in some 'unwise' sentiments onto your PC or smartphone and instantly activate the 'thought police', who are continuously monitoring the 'information superhighway' for dissenters to the politically correct narratives out there. How can Christians provide a witness for their faith under such a climate? I suggest two approaches.

1. Carry on as before doing the best that you can following your conscience and the leading of the Holy Spirit. Christians have traditionally operated in this way and many still do, particularly in the developing world, despite the penalties and often fatal outcomes, with prison and even martyrdom awaiting. This may, indeed, be the fate of some of us in our current society, if things should progress into a more sinister direction, as predicted by many an end-times preacher, sometimes in the hope that they, personally, would be 'raptured away' before things got too hot.

2. There is the holistic approach mentioned earlier and perhaps the central thesis of this book. Rather than 'talk Jesus' we proactively 'become Jesus'. Rather than judging others of the sins that will drag them to hell, we live out our faith and allow our example (and our words) to tempt them into a better way that will lead them to heaven. There's the famous saying, incorrectly attributed to Francis of Assisi, *"preach the Gospel at all times, and if necessary use words"*. Of course, as this quote demonstrates, this is all nothing new as there must have been many – and are still many – who live out their faith to such a degree that Christ pours out of every inch of their being and the Christian life becomes unshakingly compelling. These are simply people who

are living their life *Hebraically*, as a faith-driven lifestyle, rather than in the Greek mindset, that concentrates on knowledge and *doctrines about the lifestyle we should all be leading*. And, also, we must not forget that 'faith comes by hearing, and hearing by the word of God', so our deeds must also be accompanied by our words.

The way the World is going, the first option is surely going to get you into some sort of trouble. I have watched a video of a traditional street preacher who has been confronted by the police because complaints were made by some of his (Biblical) language concerning homosexuals and the homeless. These people felt victimised, so he was told. He decided to go on the attack and declared that, just by using his basic human right of free speech, he too felt victimised by the 'victims' and wanted to take it further. On the one hand this is quite clever and turns the (bad) law against itself, but, on the other hand, would Jesus had done this, particularly as the preacher was quite insistent and, despite quoting from the Word of God, his combative attitude was witnessed by a lot of people?

We all need to be prepared for these kind of situations, though many of us need to pray for courage to cope with the implications. In Tudor times it was doctrine that got you into trouble, whether you were Catholic or Protestant. It really didn't matter how you behaved, or how you were modelling Jesus, it was all about your views on the Pope, or the Virgin Mary or the sacraments. Living a Christ-centred life was not going to spare you from the chopping block. These days it is not one's view of God that will get you into trouble, but rather your views on the plethora of 'victim groups' manufactured by the manipulators of our culture.

Today people do not live by doctrine or dogma except the P.C.-manufactured doctrine of 'tolerance for all' (except for 'intolerant' Christians). This gives us a challenge and an opportunity. We are called, basically, to 'fill a vacuum' once we have cleared away all the pockets of bad air. We are to break down incorrect belief. Such a task is akin to that undertaken by those brave souls who counsel those rescued from cult groups. We are called to build up, layer by layer, expressions of Biblical truth. And we are to build this in, what is, today, a thoroughly paganised culture.

In the light of this, here is my suggestion; *we don't give them ammunition for their antagonism towards us.* Just as Jesus cleverly deflected his detractors, by turning their words against them, we too must learn to deflect, without compromising our position.

We can deflect by leaving all the judging to God Himself, as the Bible tells us.

"If anyone hears my words but does not keep them, I do not judge that person. For I did not come to judge the world, but to save the world." (John 12:47)

"Do not judge, or you too will be judged. For in the same way you judge others, you will be judged, and with the measure you use, it will be measured to you." (Matthew 7:1-2)

When you re-examine many of the cases handled by, for example, *Christian Concern*, the antagonists have felt judged in some way. In the usual way we do our evangelism this is unavoidable because, *how can we help people to be convicted of their sins if they don't realise they are sinners in the first case?*

Well … perhaps it is not our job? Jesus spoke here about the coming of the Holy Spirit:

"When he comes, he will prove the world to be in the wrong about sin and righteousness and judgment: about sin, because people do not believe in me; about righteousness, because I am going to the Father, where you can see me no longer; and about judgment, because the prince of this world now stands condemned." (John 16:8-11)

The Holy Spirit will convict souls. Perhaps that means that we should leave this to him. Rather than accusing people as 'sinners' we demonstrate that, as 'sinners' ourselves, we have overcome its power and have moved into a life of real purpose and hope accordingly?

So, we turn the focus from them ... to ourselves. Let's remind ourselves of our six 'rules' we would seek to encourage in converts and tweaking them to reflect ourselves.

- Accepting Jesus as our model.
- Demonstrating Jesus living inside us.
- Not just reflecting Jesus, but honouring God and engaging with the Holy Spirit.
- Showing Godly wisdom in our decision making.
- Seeking to honour others and working for the benefit of others.
- Demonstrating our role in God's kingdom.

So, how does this work in our evangelism and in our everyday life of living as a Christian in the World? Let us be, first, buoyed up by Scripture.

Therefore, since through God's mercy we have this ministry, we do not lose heart. Rather, we have renounced secret and shameful ways; we do not use deception, nor do we distort the word of God. On the contrary, by setting forth the truth plainly we commend ourselves to everyone's conscience in the sight of

God. And even if our gospel is veiled, it is veiled to those who are perishing. The god of this age has blinded the minds of unbelievers, so that they cannot see the light of the gospel that displays the glory of Christ, who is the image of God. For what we preach is not ourselves, but Jesus Christ as Lord, and ourselves as your servants for Jesus' sake. For God, who said, "Let light shine out of darkness," made his light shine in our hearts to give us the light of the knowledge of God's glory displayed in the face of Christ. (2 Corinthians 1-6)

Let us work through our six rules and see how they can help us to connect with a World gone mad. Firstly ... Jesus himself.

Jesus our model

16

Accepting Jesus as our model is, after all, surely the goal of every Christian:

And we all, who with unveiled faces contemplate the Lord's glory, are being transformed into his image with ever-increasing glory, which comes from the Lord, who is the Spirit. (2 Corinthians 3:18)

We have to embrace our *Hebraic* natures. It is His desire that we are transformed into the likeness of Jesus, which means that ideally the World should see us as a collection of 'little Jesuses'. This is a Hebraic imperative, flowing freely from Holy Scripture, yet has been overhauled by the Greek insistence of *argument, not action!*

We are called to 'buck the trend'. For every William Wilberforce there's a Jefferson Davis, the confederate President who said that slavery was established by decree of Almighty God. For every Mother Teresa there's a Creflo Dollar who insists that poor people are under a curse. For every pontificating coffee shop philosopher glorying in his own wisdom there's the faithful church volunteer dishing out food for the poor. We must not just be out there doing God's work, but to be seen doing it, so that He gets the Glory. We must demonstrate 'the gap', mentioned earlier, the difference between those who represent the Kingdom of Heaven and those who are bound up in the World.

Here's a way we can start to shatter a typical

stereotype bandied about by the media, that of the sour-faced, judgemental Christian. Here's a famous quote from Hosea to get us started:

For I desire mercy, not sacrifice, and acknowledgment of God rather than burnt offerings. (Hosea 6:6)

Jesus considered this important enough to reinforce:

... Jesus said, "It is not the healthy who need a doctor, but the sick. But go and learn what this means: 'I desire mercy, not sacrifice. For I have not come to call the righteous, but sinners'" (Matthew 9:12-13).

How many Christians do we know who busy themselves doing 'good works', usually in a very public, visible manner, in order to demonstrate 'living out their faith'? We have all done this at certain times, me included. There is sacrifice involved, of time or money or reputation perhaps. I'm not knocking this if the motive is pure, that is, that it comes from mercy rather than sacrifice. If the motive is to perform a sacrifice, then self-righteousness can be the real motive. What God prefers is that the act is motivated by mercy, love and an outpouring from the heart.

And the reason I mention this is that those watching can usually read us. It can be in the facial expressions, or body language, or in words spoken. *They can tell if it's look at me doing my Christian duty. I don't really want to do this but I'm trying to show you what Christians do.* This doesn't impress, this is Dot Cotton (Eastenders) in a soup kitchen, or Mrs Mangel (Neighbours) in a homeless shelter. It can paint a picture of a demanding God driving His reluctant troops forward.

What they should be seeing is Jesus, acting out of love and mercy, an individual exhibiting the fruits of the spirit ... *love, joy, peace, forbearance, kindness, goodness,*

faithfulness, gentleness and self-control (Galatians 5:22-23)
... rather than the fruits of their labour ... *grimaces, puffing and panting, self-satisfaction and pride.*

Many Christians are happy to perform acts of self-righteousness yet, in their daily dealings with others, show none of the spiritual fruits listed above and compel people to wonder, *is there really anything different about this person. What's so special being a Christian anyway?* Let's remind ourselves:

And we all, who with unveiled faces contemplate the Lord's glory, are being transformed into his image with ever-increasing glory, which comes from the Lord, who is the Spirit. (2 Corinthians 3:18)

If we are to truly contemplate the Lord's glory then aren't we glimpsing the face of Jesus and wondering whether others see the same when they look at us? The best we can do is examine all of the popular Christian stereotypes and boldly declare *not on my watch!*

We have just mentioned the sour-faced judgemental Christian. This one has been answered. We need to perform our acts out of love and mercy, not duty and sacrifice, with the spiritual fruits at the fore. We must also learn not to judge, but leave that to the Holy Spirit working through the conscience of others. We are to accentuate the positives in our own lives as a yardstick and pray that we *may provoke some to jealousy.*

Then there's the stereotypical soppy cleric with buck-teeth, dog collar and little grasp of the real world. Think of the Rowan Atkinson vicar in *Four Weddings and a Funeral* or Derek Nimmo (for really old 'uns). This has been the face of liberal ineffectual Christianity ever since the early days of radio. It is still around and these people are reeled out to make pronouncements on such hot topics as same-sex marriages to assure the World that the Church has 'moved with the times'. The reality is that they have probably long lost any role they may have once had in the Kingdom of Heaven. If this describes you or anyone you know then, be assured, there's still hope. God doesn't give up on anyone and will give you a fresh start ... as long as you get right with Him. What a witness it would be for the public to see the power of repentance and restoration in action!

If you are pure and upright, surely now He would rouse Himself for you and restore your righteous estate. (Job 8:6)

A recent media stereotype is a new staple in the world of Soaps, the *fallen vicar*. These are invariably handsome young clerics who are seduced by the flesh and abandon their calling at the drop of a hat (or a fetching pair of bloomers). An entertainment industry website has, in 2017, compiled a list of the seven sauciest soap vicars, drawing from the world of Emmerdale, Neighbours, Hollyoaks, Coronation Street, Brookside and Eastenders, with the added frisson that two of these involved gay relationships. In for a penny, in for a pound!

Sadly these stereotypes have become an increasing phenomenon in the Church in the real world, such is the allure of our permissive society, and you can be assured that every instance will be heavily trumpeted by the mainstream media. This is a terrible witness, especially if the story involves cover-ups or even compliance by church authorities, and the only way to counter this is to ensure that all clergy have a functioning accountability system that can detect these things before they have gone too far. Of course anyone caught up personally in such a drama has to weigh up pleasures of the flesh against the very real realisation that, despite the false illusion of cheap grace that abounds, *God is not to be mocked.*

Or do you not know that wrongdoers will not inherit the kingdom of God? Do not be deceived: Neither the sexually immoral nor idolaters nor adulterers nor men who have sex with men nor thieves nor the greedy nor drunkards nor slanderers nor swindlers will inherit the kingdom of God. (1 Corinthians 6:9-10)

Not many of you should become teachers, my fellow believers, because you know that we who teach will be judged more strictly. (James 3:1)

Then there are the wicked charlatans who haunt our television sets if we tune into Christian TV during one of their 'financial appeals'. The 'prosperity preachers' peddle empty promises, fed by a mangling of Scripture, and the Bible has clear warnings against this.

Those who want to get rich fall into temptation and a trap and into many foolish and harmful desires that plunge people into ruin and destruction. For the love of money is a root of all kinds of evil. Some people, eager for money, have wandered from the faith and pierced themselves with many griefs. (1 Timothy 6:9-11)

It is unbelievable to me that folk are still taken in by such nonsense, particularly those who ignore the sound advice of *once bitten twice shy.* The only people who benefit financially are – obviously – the 'preachers' themselves, as evidenced by their millionaire lifestyles! What an awful advert for the Christian faith. Even if, in some twisted way, there was once some sort of truth in their babblings, where is the faith of these preachers (some of them even calling themselves 'faith' preachers) if they fail to rely on God and His promises?

"Consider the ravens: they neither sow nor reap, they have neither storehouse nor barn, and yet God feeds them. Of how much more value are you than the birds!" (Luke 12:24)

Even in our earnestness to evangelise, we can feed the stereotype of insensitivity and inappropriateness. The Christian with the loud hailer or portable amplifier at the shopping centre or on the public highways and by-ways. They position themselves in such a way that you can't avoid them (even if it's just hearing them) and the message is often a continuous stream of scripted monologue, interspersed with Bible verses. Notwithstanding the amazing work of the Holy Spirit who can use every situation to convict the heart, the delivery mechanism is not as appropriate to our postmodern generation as in previous days. We are dealing with a generation unfamiliar and unimpressed with the Bible, so no amount of shouting or insistent tones is going to convey the truism that *this is the actual Word of God they are hearing.*

We need to consider Paul's words:

To the weak I became weak, to win the weak. I have become all things to all people so that by all possible means I might save some. I do all this for the sake of the gospel, that I may share in its blessings. (1 Corinthians 9:22-23)

Paul became all things to all men, in order to get the Gospel across in the most appropriate manner. So must we.

Finally there's perhaps the biggest stereotype of all. It's a tricky one as it is probably the closest to the truth and we have all, at some time, exhibited its characteristics. Here is the *intolerant* Christian. This is the perceived enemy of the plethora of Marxist narratives and it can never win arguments against those sucked into the postmodern politically correct fantasy of the imperialist narrow Christian antagonist. Unless we want our witness stopped in its tracks against accusations of homophobia, racism, islamophobia etc., we need to rethink the way we ... *interact with the World gone mad.* This is the purpose of this book and we have already started to touch on ways of rethinking and re-aligning ourselves, using the Hebraic model. We will start earnestly on this journey in the next Chapter. Meanwhile ...

... all of these stereotypes do nothing but harm to the Kingdom of God, as they mar the image of Jesus that is meant to shine through us to the World. They mostly demonstrate when the World, the flesh and the devil are given a foothold and are a warning for all of us to always be on our guard.

Be alert and of sober mind. Your enemy the devil prowls around like a roaring lion looking for someone to devour. (1 Peter 5:8)

So it is up to us to model the image of Jesus and, in the next Chapter, we will start to explore how ...

Following the Apostles

17

When you're unsure how to begin to tackle a massive subject, the best place to start at is the very beginning. So what I am going to do is comb through the Book of Acts and highlight every significant time the apostles *demonstrated Jesus*. Sounds like a good plan:

Then Peter said, "Silver or gold I do not have, but what I do have I give you. In the name of Jesus Christ of Nazareth, walk." Taking him by the right hand, he helped him up, and instantly the man's feet and ankles became strong. (Acts 3:6-7)

After they prayed, the place where they were meeting was shaken. And they were all filled with the Holy Spirit and spoke the word of God boldly. (Acts 4:31)

Crowds gathered also from the towns around Jerusalem, bringing their sick and those tormented by impure spirits, and all of them were healed. (Acts 5:16)

When the crowds heard Philip and saw the signs he performed, they all paid close attention to what he said. For with shrieks, impure spirits came out of many, and many who were paralyzed or lame were healed. So there was great joy in that city. (Acts 8:6-8)

As Peter traveled about the country, he went to visit the Lord's people who lived in Lydda. There he found a man named Aeneas, who was paralyzed and had been bedridden for eight years. "Aeneas," Peter said to him, "Jesus Christ heals you. Get up and roll up your mat." Immediately Aeneas got up. All those who lived in Lydda and Sharon saw him and turned to the Lord. (Acts 9:32-35)

Peter sent them all out of the room; then he got down on his knees and prayed. Turning toward the dead woman, he said, "Tabitha, get up. "She opened her eyes, and seeing Peter she sat up. (Acts 9:40-41)

Then Saul, who was also called Paul, filled with the Holy Spirit, looked straight at Elymas and said, "You are a child of the devil and an enemy of everything that is right! You are full of all kinds of deceit and trickery. Will you never stop perverting the right ways of the Lord? Now the hand of the Lord is against you. You are going to be blind for a time, not even able to see the light of the sun." Immediately mist and darkness came over him, and he groped about, seeking someone to lead him by the hand. When the proconsul saw what had happened, he believed, for he was amazed at the teaching about the Lord. (Acts 13:9-12)

In Lystra there sat a man who was lame. He had been that way from birth and had never walked. He listened to Paul as he was speaking. Paul looked directly at him, saw that he had faith to be healed and called out, "Stand up on your feet!" At that, the man jumped up and began to walk. (Acts 14:8-10)

God did extraordinary miracles through Paul, so that even handkerchiefs and aprons that had touched him were taken to the sick, and their illnesses were cured and the evil spirits left them. (Acts 19:11-12)

Paul went down, threw himself on the young man and put his arms around him. "Don't be alarmed," he said. "He's alive!" Then he went upstairs again and broke bread and ate. After talking until daylight, he left. The people took the young man home alive and were greatly comforted. (Acts 20:10-12)

There was an estate nearby that belonged to Publius, the chief official of the island. He welcomed us to his home and showed us generous hospitality for three days. His father was sick in bed, suffering from fever and dysentery. Paul went in to see him and, after prayer, placed his hands on him and healed him. When this had happened, the rest of the sick on the island came and were cured. (Acts 28:7-9)

So here we have healings, ridding of evil spirits, room shakings, raising of the dead and the blinding of an enemy. This was all done in the name of Jesus the Messiah. As we, today, worship the very same Jesus, we should be able to perform the same. Unfortunately, mostly ... we don't. How can this be? After all, Jesus gave his first group of disciples a compelling mandate:

As you go, proclaim this message: 'The kingdom of heaven has come near. Heal the sick, raise the dead, cleanse those who have leprosy, drive out demons. Freely you have received; freely give.' (Matthew 10:7-8)

So the original twelve engaged with their culture in the same way as did Paul, with the power of God manifested through them. Arguing folk into the Kingdom wasn't going to work (it never does, it's a work of the Spirit), the environment demanded Signs and Wonders.

My suspicion is that, for our current day evangelism in our current culture, Signs and Wonders, accompanied by sound apologetics and good testimony are going to be the keys to unlock the bondages imposed on the average citizen in the Western World. Yet most of us don't have these spiritual tools in our toolbox. We need to ask why not and wonder whether this is a symptom of the encroaching secularisation of society. Perhaps we have seen the same process in the

Church, *a stripping away of the supernatural*, perhaps out of fear, or perhaps out of bad teaching, or even perhaps out of a lack of faith. It looks like a baby may have been thrown out with the bathwater of fake spirituality, charismania and emotionalism of recent times. Well, ladies and gentlemen ... *I think it's time we revisited this whole subject!*

It is very Hebraic to see the spiritual in the everyday, in the World beyond the safety of our church buildings and fellowship meetings. Perhaps there's an element of fear involved, the sense of uncertainty of what the Holy Spirit may actually do if we ask him. Yet, it's all for the common good.

Now to each one the manifestation of the Spirit is given for the common good. To one there is given through the Spirit a message of wisdom, to another a message of knowledge by means of the same Spirit. (1 Corinthians 12:7-8)

A good friend is quite familiar with such things. I witnessed him in Jerusalem once receiving a series of instructions to find a specific shop in the Arab market where he was able to buy a gift for his wife at an amazingly knocked-down price. On another occasion, he identified two strangers in a packed conference room, in order to bless them financially.

So, in for a penny .... I was on a walk and decided to ask God for a 'Divine appointment'. Nothing happened, so I shrugged it off as, perhaps, not something for me. Then I received a text, from my wife. *Go and visit Norma*, she urged. My initial reaction was to ignore this as I had my own plans for the rest of the day then ... it dawned on me ... Norma was *my Divine appointment*. And indeed she was as my visit lasted 90 minutes and it was a meaningful encounter for both of us. The 'Divine nudge' was given to Monica rather than me directly, but it still became *my* experience.

This is how God works, I believe, in many creative possibilities. All we need to do is to ask Him seriously and have sufficient faith that there could very well be an answer. This should be an important facet to our evangelism, whether we are on a major campaign, or just living our life among those who are living in the World and really need to be introduced to this God of the *Divine prompting*.

There, of course, are other spiritual gifts that ought to be in our arsenal. The gift of healing is one that I mentioned in *Livin' the Life*, particularly regarding a personal experience of being used in this way:

I was first called to exercise this new 'discovery' a week later at our Foundations conference in East Anglia. As with some of the best 'God moments' it was unexpected. It was the last morning of the conference and Jo, our worship leader, invited those who needed healing to announce themselves and for people to pray for them. Usually I am too caught up with planning and 'issues' to actually partake in the activities of such times, but I was compelled – prompted by the instructions a week earlier – to pray for a young lady with muscular problems. I laid my hand on her shoulder and prayed ... and nothing happened. Then I waited for a minute or two, no idea why as I had a million and one things to attend to. Then a thought entered my mind, I recommenced the exercise and prayed that she may be released from a specific issue in her past. Something happened, perhaps only a small thing, but she said she felt the warmth flowing from my hand into her muscles and a slight change occurring. Wait a minute, I thought. This is me! Like many of you reading this book, this is not my world, this is what other people do. But the words keep coming back to me, the normal Christian life. Up to now, what was normal to me was the gathering of knowledge in order to teach it and write about it. My books and speaking engagements enabled me to distance myself from real living people. No need for me to evangelise people as my books did this for me. No need to engage people directly as I can hide behind a pulpit and allow my words to teach and convict hearts. It was all too easy, but was it really the normal Christian life? Dealing with people seemed to be what other people did. My books were my ticket away from personal involvement. To be honest, I have been deluding myself. In that moment when the young lady was affected by the Holy Spirit operating through my touch, I realised that no Christian should hide behind their own reluctance and excuses and there was real blessing in actually getting involved with people, whatever one's theology or self-importance has told you!

God has healed me three times this year of physical ailments, from the mildly irritating, to the persistent torment, to a potentially life-threatening situation. God certainly does heal today and in so many different ways and circumstances. One of my healings was a result of prayer and anointing of oil, one was a personal deal struck with my Creator and the third was totally unexpected as I hadn't even prayed about it! This is all about undeserved grace, rather than favour and all resulted in God receiving all of the glory.

I don't apologise if I have already made this point, but it's an important one. In the current climate there are thousands of voices wanting to be heard. There are also sinister controls in place to ensure that some of them will not reach their intended targets, particularly those that belong to an *unacceptable* 'narrative'. Our particular *Christian* narrative is about as unacceptable as you can get with the thought police that patrol the public arena these days. Yet we are the only people speaking up for the Kingdom of God, our narrative is 'head and shoulders' above all others just as the Name of Jesus is above all other names. We need always to be mindful of this distinctive and maintain the gap between our narrative and all others. We do this by demonstrating Jesus with all the power we have in our arsenal. Ours are not just words, they represent the very authority of God, given to us and, to drive them home, as with Jesus, as with Paul and the disciples, they need to work in conjunction with Signs and Wonders, healings, words of knowledge and wisdom.

So, there is power and there are words. Now for the words …

Words are our medium of communication and, in terms of how effectively we use them, they can either make us or break us. As we have seen in an earlier Chapter, an unwise word or phrase can even get us in trouble with the authorities, accused of a 'hate crime'. So choose them carefully, we must (as Yoda would say).

The tongue has the power of life and death ... (Proverbs 18:21)

It may be that the current P.C. climate has done us some favours by making us rethink how we 'do evangelism' and, if we add a Hebraic flavour to the mix, we may find ourselves speaking life like never before. So, here are a few ideas to mull over.

The one thing that has always engaged my interest is that the way Christians evangelise is surely informed by their doctrinal and denominational preferences. For instance, you would expect a charismatic to go about witnessing for their faith a little differently to their Lutheran friends. Does that mean that the experience of the *witnessee* will depend on the theology of the *witnesser?* It's an interesting point but also an extremely troubling point if the witnesser is a Jehovah's Witness or a Mormon, where the damage of a false conversion can be profound, with eternal consequences. In fact it would be better for them to stay in ignorance than to accept a false Christ and an empty salvation; *so much damage that would need to be undone!*

One thing that is certain in the majority of evangelism conducted in our country, is that areas controversial within the Christian world would rarely feature in discussions with unbelievers. I listed out five of these in my book, *How the Church lost the Truth*, labelling them as 'battlegrounds'; Creation, Israel, Hell, Salvation and End times. Although these are important issues, all find themselves riddled with controversy and conflict as a result of eighteen centuries of Greek thinking. This is not the place to debate the rights or wrongs of each position taken but I am going to suggest that we should not shy away from introducing them to a non-believer simply because we Christians can't agree on these positions. In fact isn't there every possibility that our adversary has a hand in this? Could it be that, discussing these 'battlegrounds' from a *Hebraic* perspective can point even clearer to a God of miracles, certainty and righteousness?

Let's consider Creation. This is such a battleground because it sits squarely on the fault line separating Science and faith. To believe in a God Who creates the Heavens and the Earth in six days is seemingly at odds with two centuries of contrary scientific evidence and no less a theologian as Tom Wright has declared that those who believe in the former are following a 'false religion'. So, is this an area best avoided if this is going to open the Gospel to ridicule? Are we asking Creationists to avoid the subject for the sake of the Gospel?

Now, the purpose of this book is not to open up such a debate, as we must remain true to our consciences and remember who the true enemy is and how he wants nothing more or less than division among

Christians. All I am suggesting is a possible approach for those who consider themselves Creationists and are unsure how this should inform their witness.

Should they not be making bold statements, particularly those that demonstrate a God Who is capable of anything, whatever scientists may say, even those of a Christian persuasion? It takes a person of unswerving faith to take such a stand but they need to be able to follow it up, to demonstrate that they are not just 'flat earthers' or 'harmless lunatics'. Scripture is needed as back up, as well as some good arguments, though Science is best avoided unless you are well versed in the alternative theories provided by Creation Science. In short, you must follow the witness put in your heart by the Holy Spirit and, sometimes, your boldness itself can provide this witness, to show that you follow a remarkable, limitless God. Never forget that we follow a person *through whom all things were created: things in heaven and on earth, visible and invisible, whether thrones or powers or rulers or authorities; all things have been created through him and for him.* (Colossians 1:16)

So here's a possible scenario:

Witnessee: You lot are living in the past. Surely our scientists have disproved a lot that you tell us, like creating the Universe in six days. That's a joke, isn't it?

Witnesser: Well, most of us Christians have moved with the times. We've realised that God used evolution to fulfil His purposes ...

Witnessee: So these Creationists don't represent what you believe?

Witnesser: Certainly not.

Witnessee: So where in the Bible does it say that God used evolution?

Witnesser: Well it doesn't, but ...

Witnessee: I thought the Bible was important to you people.

OK, so this is a bit contrived and those of you who are not Creationists may consider this a bit unfair. But the point I'm trying to make is how are we going to show that there is a massive difference between the Kingdom of God and the Kingdom of the World, if we try and have our feet in both camps? One thing about Creationism is that it is an unmistakable declaration of what camp you are in. We mustn't follow doctrines just to 'fit in' or 'be relevant', instead we must show that we are different and that we follow *a very different Way to what the World offers*. Here's how the above conversations could have gone:

Witnessee: You lot are living in the past. Surely our scientists have disproved a lot that you tell us, like creating the Universe in six days. That's a joke, isn't it?

Witnesser: Not really, it's just that we follow the Bible, even when it may seem uncomfortable. When I read the Bible I see six days ...

Witnessee: So despite all the scientific evidence, you believe that God created the universe in six days?

Witnesser: Yes and if He had done it in six microseconds that would be no problem for me either.

Witnessee: How can you say that?

Witnesser: It's just that the reason why I am taking time to talk to you about my beliefs is that I have faith in what I read in the Bible – despite what you, or Richard Dawkins, or your teachers and friends say. It's the same faith that also gives me a real hope for better things and a life of purpose, when the whole World seems to be going crazy and offering neither!

Witnessee: Well at least you're honest ... but it's not for me!

So he's probably laughing at you, but he may not forget you, *because You are bringing some strange ideas to our ears* ... (Acts 17:20)

Another 'battleground' is *Israel*. So central to God's story, but pushed to one side by a Church jealous at promises made and zealous to usurp the position of its 'older brother'. As you can imagine, a Hebraic understanding has to have a position on Israel and the Jewish people. It does, but not in the way many in the Church imagine. The key thought is that Jesus was (and still is) a Jew and, if we are to represent him, we can't strip him away from his cultural identity, just because the Church has done so in the past (and is still doing so).

If the Church could just wake up and realise how the story of God's covenant relationship with His people, Israel, has been played out in full view in history, from Biblical times to now, there is *arguably no better apologetic for God*. You may have heard the story of Frederick II of Prussia, who asked his doctor for a proof of the existence of God. *"The Jews, your majesty"*, replied the doctor. With all that has happened in history since then, with the Holocaust, the formation (and struggles) of the State of Israel and the continued blight of anti-Semitism, *this truth should be shouted from the rooftops*. The full story is in my book, *Outcast Nation* and perhaps the most telling realisation is this:

How have the Jews managed to survive so long despite being hated by so many people? Could it be that a great power has been *protecting* them and that the reason that they have been hated for so long is that another great power has been *attacking* them. This provides us with an answer to our key question. The reason the Jews have managed to survive so long despite being hated by so many people is because the power that is protecting them is *greater* than the power that has been attacking them. God against satan, the devil. No contest.

This should not just help us in our evangelism, but it should prompt us to get involved in *Jewish evangelism*. No group of people has contributed more to your individual salvation story, succinctly explained in these two passages in Romans:

For I could wish that I myself were cursed and cut off from Christ for the sake of my people, those of my own race, the people of Israel. Theirs is the adoption to sonship; theirs the divine glory, the covenants, the receiving of the law, the temple worship and the promises. Theirs are the patriarchs, and from them is traced the human ancestry of the Messiah, who is God over all, forever praised! Amen. (Romans 9:3-5)

Again I ask: Did they stumble so as to fall beyond recovery? Not at all! Rather, because of their transgression, salvation has come to the Gentiles to make Israel envious. (Romans 11:11)

For most Christians this is uncomfortable at the best of times, so the thought of introducing it to an evangelistic *spiel* is maybe one step too far. Yet the Jews' painful journey can draw people into our story in many ways:

• The holiness of God. Warnings given to them in

Deuteronomy 28 went largely unheeded and serve as a warning to all who follow their own way, rather than God's Way. The Church can draw a great lesson from this regarding its own behaviour!

• The love and faithfulness of God. The Jews have been preserved as a distinct people and have generally thrived when allowed to do so. God promised Abraham that his seeds would form a great nation and the evidence is clear for all to see.

• The fulfilment of promises. The impact that Jews have made on the World is unprecedented. A people who constitute just 0.19% of the population have produced 22% of all Nobel prize winners in the 20th century, for example!

• A reminder of spiritual battles. As already remarked, as well as providing an apologetic for the existence of God, *anti-Semitism* provides a reminder of the activities of the great adversary, satan.

• Assurance. If God can be seen to be fulfilling His promises to the Jewish people, promises made over 4,000 years ago, then He's also a God we can trust for our own salvation.

Creation and Israel sit so uncomfortably with most in the Church that they are rarely spoken about even within church walls. This is because they are counter-cultural, they go against the grain, they speak of a God greater and more involved than many in the Church allow Him to be, especially since the rise of Darwinism and 'theistic evolution' in the mid-19th century and the re-emergence of virulent anti-Semitism in the UK Church since Victorian times. Yet they speak of a great God, an awesome God of power, yet One of unbreakable faithfulness.

Hopefully you now have some more food for thought

as we seek to demonstrate and represent Jesus Hebraically, through our spiritual connections and the witness of our words. Remember, we must strive to *become Jesus* to those around us and this should be the Jesus who instructs, heals and comforts, rather than the Jesus who rails at the hypocrites and overturns the stalls of the moneychangers (he did these things because he had heavenly authority, something we need to earn in the eyes of others)! People are watching us all the time and we need to make sure that even before we open our mouths that there are no stumbling blocks of our own making.

Stumbling blocks

19

To remind us of the three golden rules mentioned earlier, we should reflect Jesus, honour God and engage with the Holy Spirit. It's the Trinity in action, as displayed by your thoughts, words and deeds. And all this must be wrapped up in a great big dollop of Godly wisdom. This should be the normal Christian life, a person fully equipped to engage with the World ... and with the enemy ... because he's not going to make it easy for you.

He's going to try to trap you with your words. That's a persistent tactic these days as those testimonies in an earlier Chapter have highlighted. And this is why our approach should be one of reflecting Jesus and the life he has given us, rather than judging the World around us, however much we are bursting to launch into a righteous diatribe!

A recent case study is supplied by an interview on *Good Morning Britain* with the MP, Jacob Rees-Mogg, in September 2017. The best way to explain it is to watch the story develop.

This first question came right out of the blue, with no build up. My comments are italicised.

Susanna Reid: What are your views on same-sex marriage?

(So she goes straight for the jugular and, by doing so, follows the standard Cultural Marxism script for discrediting any public figure who claims to have a Christian faith).

Jacob Rees-Mogg: I am a Catholic and I take the teachings of the Catholic Church seriously. But marriage is a sacrament and the decision of what is a sacrament lies with the Church and not with parliament.

(What has usually been considered a complaint about politicians actually works well in Rees-Mogg's favour here – the ability to avoid answering a straight question. He deflects it by referring to his higher authority, that happens to be the Catholic faith, rather than Jesus, in his case).

SR: OK. Does that mean you oppose same-sex marriage?
(Persistence here, in the hope that he will slip).

JRM: I support the teaching of the Catholic Church.
(Standard politician's response – repeating the previous answer).

SR: Can I repeat, do you oppose same-sex marriage?
(Yet again …)

JRM: I support the teaching of the Catholic Church.
(Yet again …)

Piers Morgan: Do you oppose same-sex marriage?
(Morgan weighs in, rather more insistently in his tone of voice).

JRM: The teaching of the Catholic Church is perfectly clear. Marriage is the important thing. This is not how people arrange their lives. It's that marriage is a sacrament and sacraments are of the authority of the Church and not the State. This is exactly the argument that Thomas More made at the opposition of the marriage of Henry VIII and Anne Boleyn.

(He is not to be defeated and brings in a historical

heavyweight to back himself up).

SR: So religion plays a big part in your politics? Do you think gay sex is a sin?

(Realising that he's far too wily an interviewee, she again goes for the jugular).

JRM: On the issue of sin it is quite clear in the teaching of the Church that it is not for me to judge. I very strongly feel that I should not judge what other people do. If you look at the woman taken in adultery, what does Christ say, that he who is without sin should cast the first stone. It is not for me to …

(A great answer and probably a practiced one. He's sticking to his guns).

PM: You have used your Catholic belief to - rather than say you oppose same-sex marriage – you say you support the Catholic church's teaching on the subject. The Catholic church believes that gay sex is a sin so I don't think it is unreasonable to ask you – as indeed Tim Farron was asked – and it caused him great damage – just a straight question, do you think it is a sin?

(Although Morgan knew that the less-canny Tim Farron's direct answer did for his political career at the highest level, he is offering him the same 'honourable death'. Did he really expect him to fall for this one?)

JRM: I have answered the straight question that the teaching of the Church in matters of faith and morals is authoritative and it is equally a teaching of the Church that it is not to me to judge others …

SR: If you were Prime Minister would the teachings of the Church take precedence over your political views?

JRM: These matters in the House of Commons are free votes, they are not party votes as they are not the issue of party politics.

SR: But you are someone tipped to lead a party, to potentially become Prime Minister of a multi-faith country.
(The implication is that a practicing Christian is an unsuitable candidate for the highest office. This is the sad state of our country!)

JRM: None of these issues are party issues they are issues decided by parliament on free votes .... Why I am emphasising the teachings of the Church is that I want to make it clear that I am supporting something not opposing something. I don't want to criticise people who lead lives that are different to mine but equally I don't want to divert from the historic teaching of the Catholic church.

PM: What's your view on abortion?
(Again, defeat leads to a fresh attack. This one does unfortunately result in direct answers, controversial enough in our climate for a swathe of newspaper headlines the following day questioning the suitability of Jacob Rees-Mogg for the highest office. So the relentless questioning does get a result and the Cultural Marxists were presumably wringing their hands in glee).

Later on, after being grilled in a similar manner on abortion issues, he remarked with great resignation, *I thought I was on here to speak about Brexit!*

What can we learn from this short exchange? There's good and there's bad. Rees-Mogg was right to refer to a higher authority, rather than taking on the mantle of judge himself. Unfortunately it's not good practice for us to refer to the Church as our higher authority, as otherwise we are suddenly answerable for all the bad things the Church has been responsible for and is still responsible for.

Our higher authority can only be *Jesus himself*, unplugged, unadorned and without any added flavours. And to do this effectively we need to model him, as we have already explored. We need to speak as he did, act as he did and think as he did.

Could we have done any better than Rees-Mogg? Probably not, but we can certainly learn from him, in principle, in two ways:

• By not incriminating ourselves with our words.

There is wisdom needed here, because there will be situations where a direct approach is needed. Jesus certainly knew when to answer difficult questions directly, when it suited him. He was always in charge of the occasion. We need to be too and if it means that we are tuned into God's Wisdom rather than our own, then so be it. We are not politicians, but we have access to a Greater Mind. We just need to be trained to hear His Voice.

• By appealing to a higher authority.

If the higher authority is Jesus, then we are bound by his words and deeds, which puts us on safe, yet dangerous ground. It is safe because we can trust him but it is dangerous because his voice is not a welcome one in today's climate. If our higher authority is our church then we are answerable for all that the Church has said and done and, at the hands of a canny 'adversary', we may find ourselves on very shaky ground, having to answer such questions as, *why does your 'Church' own so much land and investments and why was it silent during the Holocaust?*

But, if we take the initiative, surely there is more we can do. Rees-Mogg could have asked his inquisitors whether they would be asking the same questions of faith to Sadiq Khan, the Muslim mayor of London, knowing full well that this would not fit the 'narrative' of the protection of multiculturalism as a 'victim group'.

As we saw in an earlier Chapter, Jesus was most effective when he took control and directed the flow of the conversation. Here is such an interaction between Mike, a friend of mine, and a visitor to a New Age fair. This is a close approximation to the conversation, as I don't remember the *exact* words:

Mike: Do you believe in a higher power?

Lady: Yes I do. It's an angel that speaks to me and advises me.

Mike: So this angel is your higher power then? Your God?

Lady: Yes.

Mike: And is this angel clever and wise? What I mean is do you think he is cleverer than you are?

Lady: Yes, of course. This is why he helps get me through life.

Mike: But if he's that clever …. How do you know he isn't tricking you, that he may not actually be working for your best interests?

Lady: I just … know …

Mike: Because, if he's cleverer than you, then surely he can tell you anything, even if it's not going to do you any good. Who told you that he's to be trusted?

Lady: (pauses) He did …

Mike: Now let me tell you who I trust … and

why …

This is an actual encounter and Mike was able to zero into a flaw in her thinking and create a tiny chink of uncertainty, to allow him to pour in some truth into her life. He was tapping into Godly wisdom and rather than just steaming in with the Gospel, he created an opening for himself.

Here's another example of the pitfalls of appearing on live TV, presenting a case that, just a year or two ago, would have been met with sympathy and respect. Boy, have things changed! Here is a teacher, Joshua Sutcliffe, who has been suspended and faces the sack for mistakenly calling a group of girls "girls", when one of them self-identified as a "boy". He is being interviewed by popular presenters, Philip Schofield and Holly Willoughby on ITV's *This Morning*, along with Andrea Williams, his advocate from Christian Concern. Here's the gist of their discussion

Joshua Sutcliffe: … I wanted to incorporate her into the class …

Philip Schofield: Him!

JS: Of course this is the issue isn't it, we don't know …

PS: Do you find it difficult to say 'Him'?

PS: … you said 'the issue lies with the fact that recognising gender fluidity conflicts sharply with my religious beliefs. It's not unreasonable to call someone a girl if they are born … a girl.' And that in itself could lead you straight back in the fire because that is not the way now that we are led to believe how we are to be addressing children.

JS: Our policies should be influenced by biology and

law rather than what I would say is an ideology.

Andrea Williams: ... we are changing the whole of the school policy (for a few who are afflicted) where we should be taking those pupils aside and work out how we can help them.

PS: What do you mean helping them? Cure them?

AW: If we force everyone else to conform to their gender identity then ...

PS: Children do kill themselves over this ...

AW: Suicide rates are the same for those who go through this process, compared to those who don't.

PS: You're both Christians? It doesn't seem very 'Christian' for you to be so intransigent.

AW: We are born in the image of God, male and female ... in a society that is confused, that is a fantastic message of hope. It is something that society is crying out for. The kindest thing you can do for a little child that is gender confused is to help them to live in the body that they have.

JS: The students don't really know how to react to this situation.

PS: Shouldn't you be teaching them? Isn't that your job?

Holly Willoughby: The role of the teacher is not just teaching them their subject ...

PS: Pastoral care ...

AW: Not for something that's not a reality.

PS: Are you saying that transgenderism is not a reality?

AW: The fact of a girl suddenly presenting herself as a boy is not a truth.

PS: In your eyes it's not possible to be born in the wrong body?

AW: No, we are born male and female. Surgery can't change that. The kindest thing is to help the child to live in the body that they have.

PS: If they were homosexual, would you help them not to be homosexual?

AW: It's not good for them to live in such a lifestyle. It's not good for our children to be highly sexualised.

PS: I am finding this utterly abhorrent!

PS: ... and you are in direct conflict with your own church *(Church of England – which had just released some pro-LGBTIQ+ rulings).*

AW: This was an opportunity for the Church to point to the most compassionate and beautiful person that has ever walked ... (INTERRUPTIONS BY HW) ... Jesus Christ ...

PS: (interrupting) Back to the show and back to 2017 and not just medieval Britain ...

Of course this was just the gist, but all words above were actually spoken. Without seeking to be disparaging to Philip Schofield personally, we can see him as a typical example of someone of high profile in the media who is expected to reflect the postmodern, Cultural Marxist narrative, as we have explored throughout this book. Let us look forensically at four statements that Schofield made in this exchange:

... *because that is not the way now that we are led to believe* ...

Are we just sheep being led by wolves? Why should we be led anyway? Who is doing the leading and what is their agenda? It gives every impression of cultish behaviour, where others impose their beliefs on us and we blindly accept them!

... It doesn't seem very 'Christian' for you to be so intransigent ...

How sad it is that society has confused 'being Christian' with being accepting. The truth is in fact the complete opposite. This is the sad legacy of 'political Christianity' trying to appease the World by 'being relevant'.

... I am finding this utterly abhorrent! ...

Strong words, strong emotions. This whole issue has been led by emotions - not facts or rational debate. This is an important issue. We are going to find many current debates on issues pertaining to 'victim culture' driven by *emotions* and not by logic. People are going to respond to you or attack you with flimsy arguments fuelled with an emotional, even quasi-religious, intensity that many of them don't even realise they possess. Surely this is a false emotionalism, created and fed by the media, commentators and others who have been dragged into this twilight zone. People are going to feel strongly about issues such as immigration, islamophobia or gender fluidity without knowing why. The delusion is far-reaching and we are even going to find many Christians pulled into this. What can we do? Follow this variation of the old wartime adage, Keep calm and ... *don't get upset or provoked!* We need this calmness, we need to pray against our emotions running away with us. It will be difficult, but it's going to be necessary, as fighting emotions with emotions will just produce an emotional mess, not a reasoned debate, *and hearts and minds will remain untouched!*

... Back to the show and back to 2017 and not just

medieval Britain …

Andrea Williams has done us a great service by distancing true Christianity from the compromised position held by the Church of England, even if we are seen as outdated and 'medieval'.

Reaching a World gone mad is going to require more Godly Wisdom, rather than relying on our own powers of articulation or knowledge and experience. Each encounter will have its own challenges, particularly if the enquirer has an ulterior motive (and a knowledge of the laws of the land).

Yet there are other ways of communication, that do require the ability to string together some intelligible words in an entertaining way, to say nothing of knowledge and wisdom … the lost art of *storytelling*, known as agada in Hebraic thought and tradition. Agada is at the heart of being human, which can be a good or a bad thing. It depends on the quality of the story, teaching or interpretation and whether it gives glory to God by pointing to truths in His revealed Word. As a kid I remember David Kossoff, the Jewish storyteller, who was often on TV reading his Bible tales. Without putting any significance on the fact that he was a Jew, the scenario of a wise old man sitting on a chair drawing his audience into these Bible stories is comfortably nostalgic and makes me wish that we had a few more of these storytellers in our current generation (though I doubt if they would get any TV airtime these days).

Storytelling is indeed a lost art, lost among the noise of clattering games consoles, YouTube diatribes and endless streams of trivia pouring out of our smartphones and tablets and reverberating around our skulls, drilled into our brains by the ever-present headphones. Don't we often pine for quieter, less frantic times, where the only intrusion would be the small black and white screen in the corner of the room and the transistor radio, with 'off' buttons? You would sit as a family around the dining room table and Grandad would start telling one of his tales ...

My son, Simon, works with the Chelsea pensioners, British army veterans who fought for our country in the Second World War and later conflicts. They love nothing more than to corner you and regale you with one of their stories. There's a big difference between watching a collection of pixels on a TV screen or hearing immaculate sound through Bose speakers, and sitting next to a live human being, who has lived a life and wishes to share it with you. You will be sharing an unedited moment that cannot be recorded or rewound. It could be long-winded, rambling and repetitive, but it is real and, between Adam and Eve and the dawn of the 20th century AD, that's all people had. We miss this terribly, but most of us don't realise it.

Jesus, of course, was a master storyteller, through his *parables*. He wove together truth-soaked tales of idiotic builders, shiny lamps, wayward sheep, devious servants and canny managers. They were good stories, cleverly told and enigmatic to most, their meanings becoming clear once the Kingdom of Heaven took hold of the heart.

In our task of becoming 'little Jesuses' we should, according to the giftings given to us, try to develop a good storytelling style, even if it is just to convey our 'conversion' testimony. It will allow our personality to shine, which, if nothing else, should demonstrate that Christians are not the dour, lifeless, sour-faced, atmosphere-sucking wraiths they are made out to be but are visible, living embodiment of Romans 14:17:

For the kingdom of God is not a matter of eating and drinking, but of righteousness, peace and joy in the Holy Spirit.

Role models 20

There was a day in our country, perhaps a generation or two ago, when prominent Christians were afforded a degree of respect rather than suspicion. There's a remarkable YouTube video from December 1970 when Joan Bakewell interviewed Dr. Martyn Lloyd Jones (It's at https://www.youtube.com/watch?v=-vbydx95tVQ). At that time she was a secular media personality (labelled the 'the thinking man's crumpet') and he was probably the highest profile evangelical in the UK. Although not a Christian herself, she was respectful and allowed him much space for describing the Biblical view of the sorry spiritual state of mankind. There was no inquisitorial 'Susannah Reid' intervention here, (Do you believe in same-sex marriage? Is homosexuality a sin?) but an intelligent discussion, where the viewer was provided with a clear Christian message. This type of programme would be unacceptable on British TV today and Dr. Lloyd Jones would be labelled a 'religious bigot'.

There are no prominent Christians in our current society, apart from the political clerics in the Church of England, who wander around in their robes and are good for the odd crusty sound-byte. In our 'Post Christian' society we are an endangered species aside from our holy enclosures and 'safe spaces'. In fact it would take a brave soul to raise his or her head above the parapet and offer a relevant uncompromised Biblical worldview among the bloggers and chatterers of our Mainstream Media (MSM). It would be as if a target was painted on their head, a living specimen of the 'colonial', 'oppressive' class of 'religious bigot' who is the eternal enemy of the growing hotchpotch of 'victims' and 'snowflakes' who clutter up our social marketplace. Brave? Foolhardy? But ... perhaps ... necessary. There are Biblical precedents in the Old Testament of Jews who not only were seeking to honour others but also worked for the benefit of others, even those in the Kingdom of the World.

Nehemiah was one such person. He was a high official in the Persian Court of King Artaxerxes I and in fact he had the ear of the King. Here's the single verse that establishes this:

I was cupbearer to the king. (Nehemiah 1:11)

Here is a man, living openly as a Jew in a foreign land, under a pagan government, who, not only had the ear of the King, but also had favour with the King.

"I had not been sad in his presence before, so the king asked me, "Why does your face look so sad when you are not ill? This can be nothing but sadness of heart." I was very much afraid, but I said to the king, "May the king live forever! Why should my face not look sad when the city where my ancestors are buried lies in ruins, and its gates have been destroyed by fire?" The king said to me, "What is it you want?" Then I prayed to the God of heaven, and I answered the king, "If it pleases the king and if your servant has found favor in his sight, let him send me to the city in Judah where my ancestors are buried so that I can rebuild it." Then the king, with the queen sitting beside him, asked me, "How long will your journey take, and when will you get back?" It pleased the king to send me; so I set a time." (Nehemiah 2:1-6)

So here we have a King offering to not only release

his servant to embark on an expedition to a foreign land and even write letters and send some soldiers along, to ensure a safe passage, but to do this as a purely altruistic act, without any possible advantage to himself. Not the usual actions of a King of a mighty Empire. This is true favour. Nehemiah must have made a good impression, perhaps the Jews of that day were a favoured people, rather than a despised minority. Where are the Christian Nehemiahs today, who can gain respect and favour with the secular authorities through their own standing with their God?

Then there was *Joseph*, the son of Jacob who was thrown down a well by his jealous brothers, but was rescued and ended up as the highest official in the land of Egypt, because of his ability to interpret dreams. He always made it clear as to his identity and the God that he served:

Then Pharaoh said to Joseph, "Since God has made all this known to you, there is no one so discerning and wise as you. You shall be in charge of my palace, and all my people are to submit to your orders. Only with respect to the throne will I be greater than you." (Genesis 41:39-40)

Joseph the Hebrew became the equivalent of the Prime Minister of Egypt. Again we have favour and this favour was by virtue of the God that Joseph served, a God who Pharaoh evidently respected. Joseph had proved the power of this God and that was good enough for Pharaoh. Where are the Christian Josephs today, who can gain respect and favour with the secular authorities through the demonstration of God's Wisdom?

Finally, perhaps the most pertinent example of all, *Daniel*. He was one of the capable young Jewish men, along with Meshach, Shadrach and Abednego, selected to serve in King Nebuchadnezzar's palace. They were allowed to live according to Jewish customs and were valued for their wisdom and insights and, in Daniel's case, for his ability – as with Joseph – to interpret dreams. After his first success, Daniel was made ruler of the province of Babylon and continued to live in the royal court.

Here was a man with much favour. He continued in favour with the next Babylonian ruler, King Belshazzar, interpreting the vision of the writing on the wall. For this he was proclaimed the third highest ruler in the land by a King who was slain that very night, making way for King Darius. Again Daniel was given favour and was on the verge of being proclaimed as administrator of the whole kingdom when ... some rival administrators acted out of jealousy and plotted his downfall. They played the 'religious' card, tricking the King into signing a decree to punish any who worships a foreign God. Reluctantly, the King had Daniel thrown into the lions' den. This he survived and ensured his good standing with not just Darius, but with Cyrus, the next King.

Where are the Christian Daniels today, who can gain respect and favour with the secular authorities through the demonstration of God's Wisdom and Power?

Let's consider this. In Joseph, Nehemiah and Daniel's day, Jews were not specifically hated and there was an open acknowledgement that their God was *a little bit special*. This was demonstrated by Joseph's action and particularly Daniel's actions, his faith being tested in the lions' den.

These days, there is every sense of our Western culture being *the very Lion's den*, not that place of physical danger but rather the abode of our enemy: *Your enemy the devil prowls around like a roaring lion looking for someone to devour.* (1 Peter 5:8)

Any Christian who is willing and bold enough to stand up and be counted is going to be thrown to the other lions ... the commentators, critics, bloggers, gossipers, the front-line of the anti-Christian Marxist culture that has spread to every corner of our social and political landscape. It's probably even worse than that. With a 'Church' that is far from unified and consistent, it is doubtful if such a prominent Christian voice is going to be acceptable for all of us (unless he is the antichrist who is going to fool all of us, but I'm not going there!) as there are so many varieties with over 40,000 denominations, that one size will not fit all, unless squabblings are put aside in favour of Christian unity.

Nevertheless we should pray that some of our current (or future) crop of Christian leaders are going to venture into the 'lion's den' and have not just the faith and courage, but also Godly wisdom to gain favour with them. We mustn't forget that command in Titus 2:15, *do not let them despise you.* Can you imagine the impact of public acts of signs and wonders, particularly those that can't be explained as tricks with mirrors or CGI? The hardened cynics would always cling to their disbelief, but it's not them we should be concerned about, but rather the 98% of fallen humanity who have desperate need of salvation, without a clue not just on how to be saved, but also on *why they need to be saved.*

I tell you, now is the time of God's favor, now is the day of salvation. We put no stumbling block in anyone's path, so that our ministry will not be discredited. Rather, as servants of God

we commend ourselves in every way: in great endurance; in troubles, hardships and distresses; in beatings, imprisonments and riots; in hard work, sleepless nights and hunger; in purity, understanding, patience and kindness; in the Holy Spirit and in sincere love; in truthful speech and in the power of God; with weapons of righteousness in the right hand and in the left; through glory and dishonor, bad report and good report; genuine, yet regarded as impostors; known, yet regarded as unknown; dying, and yet we live on; beaten, and yet not killed; sorrowful, yet always rejoicing; poor, yet making many rich; having nothing, and yet possessing everything.
(2 Corinthians 6:2-10)

This is not a game, it's the real world. Christian witness, whether it's from brave leaders speaking truth into the public information highways, or from individuals trying to make a difference in the environment they occupy. Persecution is not just going to be of the 'naming and shaming' variety or the 'I can't wear my cross to work' variety, but could very well begin to resemble the real physical hardships suffered by the Church in the Muslim world or in places like China or North Korea.

It would be nice if God could send His angel to shut the mouths of the lions, but this is not a likely scenario. Instead we should strive to be God's mouthpiece, that God's angels will open our mouths and give us the words to say and that, through our witness, the lions may be occasionally stunned into silence.

Reaching a World gone mad

21

It is time to get serious and think about our role in this strange and disturbing new world we find ourselves in. The need for the uncompromised Christian gospel has never been greater, especially as many even in the Church have been infiltrated by Cultural Marxist ideas. It has often been too subtle for them to realise but perhaps this book can act as a wake-up call for them, telling them that there is still time to get your house in order. But first we need to get back to basics, to the *Church of Jesus Christ*, rather than the 'Church of a re-imagined Jesus for the 21st century'.

So what can we do? What can we do *differently?* Here are some thoughts for starters, based on what we have learned so far.

• The World has changed enormously since the 1960s and this has accelerated over the last couple of years. The biggest fundamental change has been attitudes towards what is true and what is false. Truth is not a major concern in our postmodern culture and certainly not objective truth. This must be the primary evidence that we are living in a post-Christian 'brave new World'.

• We are in a situation of very real opposition – perhaps even irrationally so – to the Gospel because of its perception as an authoritarian aggressor and representing an 'anti-progressive' agenda.

• Because of the first two points above, the default

mindset of people in the UK is one of confusion and hopelessness. The key is whether people are content to remain so or whether they are open-minded enough to break out of the torpor and search for the real meaning in life that they have been denied. We, of course, know that there is only one place where this real meaning can be found.

We are therefore presented with real challenges. Of course nothing is beyond the ability and scope of the Holy Spirit but there's a suspicion that He acts in response to the spiritual state of the Church, which is currently not very healthy. I believe that there are two solutions to the current sorry state, a corporate solution and an individual one.

Corporately … the Church needs to get onto its knees and repent of the distance it has allowed itself to fall since the Church of the original apostles (some of these are adapted from the list I provided in *Hebraic Church*):

• The structures and hierarchies it has created, distancing itself from the simple purity of the original Church.

• The unity it has lost, with empire building within the Church a reflection of worldly attitudes. Where is there true integration between black and white churches, for instance?

• Anti-semitism, still a major problem in the UK Church. Anti-Israelism is just a different way of expressing this. Jesus must be understood from within his Jewish context.

• Division through a Greek emphasis on argument, rather than the Hebraic imperative of fellowship.

• There needs to be sufficient faith in God to really

believe that He still speaks to us today and is capable of doing more than the scientists limit Him to.

• We need a higher view of the Bible as God's means of communication to us, rather than a rubber-stamp for our own particular views. An understanding that God's revelation to us in the Old Testament is still important and has not been superseded.

• Where is the LIFE? The joy has mostly been stripped out of our Christian life, transforming us from an outwardly thankful and worshipful community of the redeemed to a dour, irrelevant, inwardly-looking ghetto.

Individually ... we need to consider some new ways (or even some old ways but better thought out). Here are some ideas for starters ...

The Media

We should be feeding into the media universe rather than drawing from it, unless we are discerning enough to find sources that are agenda-free (unless, of course, it is a Christian agenda). Our evangelism and outreaches in the world of the media is not any more something we can leave to the 'professional' Christian ministries with big budgets and resources. The web, for all of its faults, provides us with unprecedented opportunities. For instance, this book would have been impossible without the web, particularly in finding dependable alternative viewpoints on YouTube (see Appendix B).

Technology is getting cheaper and cleverer all the time. It is now possible to broadcast live video from your PC (or even your smartphone), with a dozen or so other people simultaneously, without paying a penny. The potential for this is incredible. We currently use the

Zoom service (www.zoom.us) to enable us to run interactive Bible studies and also running a regular live video news panel online. This is not rocket science in terms of technology or skills. Think about a scenario where you can create a similar service for your local community online. Three or four of you could form a web panel (all from different locations) and you can chat about issues of interest in your community, with a gentle Christian slant. This is the embryo of a local TV station. You can even record the sessions and make them viewable on demand on YouTube. It's all possible, it just needs a vision for it:

Where there is no vision, the people perish ... (Proverbs 29:18 KJV)

I mention in Appendix B those ordinary people who have done this and have actually made a career out of it. At the time of writing none of them are Christians. Could this be a ministry that is calling you?

Around ten years ago we started a web initiative called *Saffron Planet*. It consisted of around eight people sitting around a dinner table, all miked up and chatting as a group of friends do. These chats were recorded and put out as mp3 audios on a website. They are still there on www.saffronplanet.net and, when we get the time, we will return to this. It has made an impact because people listening hear a group of ordinary people talking without restriction on relevant subjects. The chats are not always explicitly Christian, but the underlying worldview is, so people understand what they are getting. It is a safe place for people to be introduced to Christianity and we are sure that many seeds have been sown over the years. The point to make is that anyone can do this, you just need the will and the organisation and, in our case, plenty of tasty food!

The web, as it stands now, bypasses the restrictions of Cultural Marxism, unless you are relying on sponsorship through YouTube, when you may hit some problems. It's a place currently without censorship and perhaps is going to be a key place for people to find an alternative worldview to that fed to them through the traditional media, particularly that which offers them hope for the future.

Personal evangelism

The Church building/gathering was never intended to be a place of evangelism. If you read the Book of Acts, you find these places are where the Church ('called out ones') comes together to encourage and build each other up.

They devoted themselves to the apostles' teaching and to fellowship, to the breaking of bread and to prayer. Everyone was filled with awe at the many wonders and signs performed by the apostles. All the believers were together and had everything in common. They sold property and possessions to give to anyone who had need. Every day they continued to meet together in the temple courts. They broke bread in their homes and ate together with glad and sincere hearts, praising God and enjoying the favor of all the people ... (Acts 2:42-47)

Evangelism was done in the synagogues, Temple courts and marketplaces, places where the people are. And so must it be with us. Perhaps it's been a cop out for far too long where we drag our friends and relatives off to the 'professional' evangelists, to crusades, missions, seeker-friendly services or other variations. This is not to say that there's not still a place for these, because God will honour our efforts and the sincere efforts of those gifted in evangelism. But, perhaps, we should step up to the plate more than we're used to. At the very least is to be mindful of this important Scripture:

Always be prepared to give an answer to everyone who asks you to give the reason for the hope that you have. (1 Peter 3:15a)

But in the context of the Hebraic mindset, the next few verses are also important:

But do this with gentleness and respect, keeping a clear conscience, so that those who speak maliciously against your good behavior in Christ may be ashamed of their slander. For it is better, if it is God's will, to suffer for doing good than for doing evil. (1 Peter 3:15b-17)

Many opportunities are going to come our way, some of them totally unexpectedly. A *clear conscience* is needed, that we have been able to model Jesus to them, not just in our words but in our body language, our tone of voice and our attitude. This is our *good behaviour in Christ*. There will be suffering and persecution, with many speaking maliciously against you, trying to trip you up, even trying to coax you into 'political incorrectness' but this suffering is a reward not a punishment, a token of our stand we are making for Christ.

Events

We have been running events over the last six years for Christians and, so far, there have been fifteen of them. They are called *Foundations*, with the by-line Faith, Family, Freedom. We originally called them 'conferences' but began to realise that the events didn't feel like a conference, yet we failed to come up with an adequate alternative moniker. I won't go into too much details as I've covered this extensively in both *Hebraic*

Church and *Livin' the Life*, but Foundations has seen many breakthroughs with people, particularly in the areas of freedom, the realising of functions and the discovery of giftings.

One thing has lately bugged me, whether the Foundations *model* could work in the context of evangelism? Could there be a situation where ordinary folk could be coaxed into a gathering that at the very least is not going to make them cringe but, ideally, is going to actually interest and excite them? The structure of Foundations is based around personal freedom, allowing folk to plot their own course, but providing them with 'building blocks' of experiences that can be part of their journey for that day. These building blocks in a Christian context have included; teaching, sung worship, dance workshops, music workshops, crafts, bible reading, show & tells, testimony, healing, yeshiva discussions, prayer walks, communion and confession. These are all human elements, the actual mechanism behind it, of course, is the *Holy Spirit* working in the life of every individual.

The key is to treat everyone as an individual, rather than as one of a herd, as we tend to do in our traditional church services. By allowing each person to have space and time, it has often resulted in meaningful 'God moments' and also a realisation of giftings that have never been discovered before, or at least encouraged. Imagine if we can work along the same lines with an unsaved friend. Rather than inclining him to see himself as a 'target' for conversion, perhaps we can build up an event as a safe place for leaving the world behind and discovering more about himself. To some this may seem a bit 'new age' or even cultish, but others may be in just the right place to try out something new.

After all, one of the abiding features of postmodernism is trying out new things (as everything has 'value'), so we may as well take advantage of this openness. Our 'un-stated' aim of course is that this can be an environment where the *Holy Spirit can do his stuff*, and so we need to make it as attractive as we can, without making false promises. The people who would possibly be attracted to this would be those who God may already be working on, in the sense of making them think hard about the *madness of the culture in which they live*.

If you're expecting me to come up with a solution that will work for you, then I'm afraid this may be a bit of a let-down. Don't depend on me but expect God to work with you on this one, so prayer is a must at this stage, as at every stage! All I can do is list a few pointers, based on our experiences:

• A discussion group relevant to the big issues of the day. A good format would be to supply copies of daily papers and encourage people to dig out relevant stories. This will need to be led by someone very tuned in to the 'zeitgeist', who can make any discussions relevant, but offering the occasional nugget with a Christian slant.

• Crafts are an excellent way to get people to open up. This can be very simple and undirected, by simply scattering around a few 'colouring in' books with pens, crayons and paints and some foolscap paper for 'doodling'. If you have skilled 'crafty' people then you can include activities such as making bookmarks, crochet or candle painting. This may seem like 'kid's stuff' but you'll be amazed how people open up, even to strangers, while their hands are busy creating things.

• Music workshops are intensely liberating even for those who have never sung or played an instrument before. You can encourage people to bring their own instrument and make a variety of percussion available. Of course, this will need to be led, to avoid a cacophony. The fact is that there are plenty of people who have learned an instrument at some time in their life but are not presented with any opportunity to play with others in a relaxed, enjoyable environment. As Foundations is all about freedom, the release this can provide can be a very liberating experience. Similarly with singing, with many good voices out there wasted in solitary bathrooms.

• *Show & Tell* is a throwback to schooldays and is an extremely popular feature at Foundations. The format is to give volunteers a ten minute slot to speak (to whoever wants to hear) on whatever they are passionate about and can include visual aids. Again, this can be most liberating and also a positive and interesting experience to hear people speaking so passionately.

• A quiet room should be made available. It should be made clear that the decision to enter the room will be 'at their own risk' because there they will find people willing to pray with/for them, counsel them and offer the possibility of healing.

The objective of all of this is not to trap people in a building, lock the doors and then get a preacher to force the Gospel down their throats. Instead it is to show Christians as ordinary folk, engaging in ordinary conversations and doing ordinary things together. If people ask questions, then 1 Peter 3:15-17 (see above) kicks in, but we should never force things. It should also be a 'safe place' free from the restrictions of the political correctness that governs the World outside.

Street evangelism / outreaches

We need to 'get out there' with our message, but how? You have heard of the traps and pitfalls and there really are people out there intent on causing mischief or worse to Christian street preachers. But that shouldn't stop us, we just need to adapt to these changing times.

Hopefully this book has already provided you with some pointers, but here are some ideas, adapted again from ideas already given in this and previous books.

- In Livin' the Life I enthused about the Healing on the Streets (HOTS) initiative that seems to have, in most cases, bypassed the pitfalls of political correctness. It does this for a very good reason in that it appeals to deepest needs, that of healing, whether physical or emotional. People need to talk to a listening ear, others need a touch of the supernatural, even if they are sceptics. At its most basic configuration this consists of a couple of chairs where people sit to be ministered to by trained volunteers, who kneel in humility before them and follow a script that covers a wide set of circumstances. This is the Gospel through the 'back door', the Word following Signs & Wonders, but the Word, when given, is always in response to what God has already done to the person, so is natural and unforced and effective.

- Any street preaching we do ideally has to follow the 'Jesus model', always mindful of what Jesus would do in the circumstance. This is a pointer to attitude, body language, tone of voice and sensitivity to situations rather than blasting away with a monologue, however well-rehearsed and Biblical. Again, there may be situations where the latter can be applicable, the key is prayer and openness to the Holy Spirit for direction. Getting into an argument with 'provocateurs' is not advisable, if you want to do that then go to 'Speakers Corner' in Hyde Park, where this is the norm and a good safe place to flex your theological muscles. Arguments over the Gospel are engaging the Greek rather than the Hebraic mindset, rationalism rather than the spiritual and there's every chance that a weak argument on your part can actually do more harm than good, bearing in mind the impressionable minds of any onlookers.

• The Foundations model mentioned in the last section could, with a bit of tweaking, be applicable in an outdoors environment, depending on the weather. Of course this may be a big challenge as it requires identifying a space where you can operate, without falling foul of the authorities, who would probably need to be forewarned. It would be a good idea to work closely with a local church, who will have local knowledge and will need to deal with any follow-up, once your work has been done. Think about a trestle table covered with daily newspapers and a lively discussion surrounding it. If relevant, this ought to be a good crowd-drawer, a carrot for the inquisitive. The key is having open interaction with people, without hijacking the situation with inappropriate preaching. Another table can have crafts. You perhaps can have a music group (with a few spare instruments) and even a trained dance group, as long as they are good. A separate area can be cordoned off as a quiet, safe place, perhaps in conjunction with a HOTS-type activity you may be running. The key to this whole enterprise is prayer and discernment, to do whatever seems right and appropriate for your audience. Always remember that your objective is to give them some sort of experience with God.

Hopefully your creative juices are stirring and ideas are beginning to flow. This Chapter is just a signpost showing the broad path, it is up to you to follow that path, if applicable, until the path becomes personal to the needs of your fellowship or church.

Being Hebraic

22

Surely madness is truly afoot. Since penning the by-line, *reaching a World gone mad*, I have seen our current culture so defined increasingly, by both Christian and secular commentators. Is it not a madness to believe that an incorrect pronoun can get you in serious trouble, that our students have become a fragile protected species, that the "n" word is more of a blasphemy these days than the variety of anti-Christian epithets that so easily roll from the tongue? That being a Biblical Christian can have you labelled as a racist or a fascist? That biological certainties have given way to subjective feelings and that the right to think this way (and the 'crime' of not thinking this way) seems to be one of the most enforced laws today?

Although the story that unfolded in the first two parts of this book may have been shocking to some, or at the very least (in typical British understatement) *quite surprising*, the solutions offered in this third part are nothing more than good Biblical common sense, I believe.

So let's remind ourselves of the main features that have been surreptitiously introduced into our society through Cultural Marxism:

> • **A mindset that believes that although humans are basically good, they are not free because of cultural oppression, that needs to be dealt with through conflict.**

This is the core principle of Marxism and we should be under no doubts that this is one of the predominant forces in our current culture. We must never forget that Christians operate differently, as citizens of the Kingdom of God, where humans are essentially depraved because of the Fall and are not free because of personal sin, which can only be dealt with by the finished work of Jesus Christ on the cross.

• **The only sinful act is one where you are the oppressor. Christians are always seen as the oppressor.**

This is a situation that feeds on division, where you are either allied with the oppressor or the oppressed. A 'victim culture' is encouraged to force people to concentrate on their 'forms' (their 'identity') rather than discovering what their 'function' is. As Christians our function is determined by our God-given purpose within the Body of Christ and our evangelism should include an assurance that everyone, ultimately, has a God-given purpose as an individual free of the labels that society is trying to stick on them.

The State is free to decide who are the oppressors and who are the oppressed and will legislate for this, removing freedom of speech in the process. The ultimate aim of Marxism is State control and we have seen where that led to in Stalinist Russia and the China of Mao Tse Tung, to say nothing of the current regime in North Korea. With the prevalence of 'victim groups' we are moving ever closer to a situation of fear and control, of guarding every word and action, in case you accidentally upset someone, particularly a member of the more *protected* minority communities. This has a serious effect on our evangelism and we must either be prepared for persecution or to find new ways of reaching people in our current culture. Being Hebraic, with mind, body and spirit working together in harmony, is suggested as the way forwards here, as this is actually only reflecting the way that Jesus and the early disciples operated.

• **The ultimate objective is to redefine the family and wrench society from its Christian roots.**

This must never be forgotten, as it was the twin aim of both the Frankfurt School and the theosophist Alice Bailey all those years ago. They knew that it wouldn't happen overnight, it was a 'long march' and our current generation was the ultimate destination. The family unit as God intended is under particular attack, with easy divorces, guilt-free sex education and the promotion of new biological definitions as to what actually constitutes a family unit. Biblical language is no longer the vocabulary of our current generation. In fact the Bible is no longer held in high esteem, so evangelism encounters new challenges. Nevertheless the abiding philosophy of postmodernism and relativism must be challenged, with *absolute truth* being defended at all costs.

• **The key driver is the creation of 'victim groups'.**

In Cultural Marxism, it is the traditional Western structure that is the oppressor and will never be allowed to forget it. The 'oppressed' are the never-ending conveyor belt of 'victim groups' created by the manipulators of the New Left. The intention is not to actually to liberate anyone, though the rhetoric is convenient. The intention is to be prejudicial to the 'oppressor' rather than to aid the 'oppressed' and thus bring about a 'Brave New World' (or a 1984). It is important though that we do not persecute or judge these 'victim groups' as they are not only pawns in the overall strategy, but in danger of being branded as instigators. They are true victims, not of the perceived 'aggressors' but *rather of the Cultural Marxists themselves*. We must not forget that Christians are not a 'victim group', neither should we seek to be, as we are 'more than conquerors' and don't need any help from Marxists as we have the Creator and the King of the Universe on our side. If some Christians believe otherwise then it is clear that they have been sucked into 'the madness' and, as with Jesus and his religious persecutors, we should be free to judge them on this, for the ultimate sake of their souls.

• **Emotionalism will triumph over rationalism.**

This is where Christians join together with traditional enemies, such as atheists and secularists, who no-doubt are in mourning over the demise of rationalistic 'modernism', superseded by the false news and emotionalism of postmodernism, with everyone seemingly following different truths and narratives. This is not rational behaviour and we are called to be rational beings, although we believe in a supernatural God. The key driver of the 'victim culture' is emotionalism, with feelings trumping all. This is just an expression of the subjectivism that it is at the heart of our new culture.

• **Identity is key.**

Cultural Marxism concentrates on the pride and

uncertainty of mankind in stressing the importance of their 'identity' over and above other 'identities', thus creating false conflicts. Our true identity is in Jesus, of course, and we should have absolutely no part in the madness that surrounds us.

• **There is no absolute truth, people have the freedom to create their own truths (as long as the State is in agreement).**

This is a summary of all we have seen above. We need to wrench people away from this falsehood as, without a grasp of an absolute truth, they will have problems responding to your evangelistic efforts.

'Do not let them despise you'.

This command in Titus 2:15 is well worth heeding if we wish to be heard by the average citizen, if not necessarily by those who 'pull the strings', who would rather we stuck to the stereotype of 'cultural aggressor'. In the Bible, Joseph, Nehemiah and Daniel rose to positions of great influence by acting honourably and consistently according to their faith. This was a remarkable witness to those in the prevailing culture.

When you see it so summarised you begin to realise what a danger we have come up against and how we need to be equipped to deal with it. I feel that the best way is to adopt a Hebraic mindset.

Despite the negative connotations implied by the word itself, being *Hebraic* is nothing more than thinking, talking and acting *Biblically*, striving to get the closest approximation to the mindset of Jesus and the apostles that 2,000 years of indoctrination into Greek thinking will allow. Our job is first to get a grip on the basic principles, so that we can grasp the underlying philosophy behind 'first generation' Christianity and then to begin to put as much of it into practice as we can. A reasonable summary is provided by the six rules developed earlier:

- Accepting Jesus as our model.
- Demonstrating Jesus living inside us.
- Not just reflecting Jesus, but honouring God and engaging with the Holy Spirit.
- Showing Godly wisdom in our decision making.
- Seeking to honour others and working for the benefit of others.
- Demonstrating our role in God's Kingdom.

In the preceding Chapters we have explored the first five and we will finish our story by thinking about what our role may be in God's Kingdom. In terms of the New Testament job centre of potential vacancies, there are plenty of *spiritual gifts* to choose from; prophesying, serving, teaching, encouraging, giving, leadership, mercy (all in Romans 12:6-8), wisdom, knowledge, faith, healing, miracles, distinguishing spirits, tongues and interpretation of tongues (added to in 1 Corinthians 12:4-11). And, of course, many of these would be subdivided and expanded, just as our current society has broadened so much since those Biblical days. Even though there is no specific spiritual gift of *writing*, I claim the gift of teaching as my implementation of this activity.

And what about the gift of evangelism? Is there no specific gift? Surely some are called to be evangelists and show great desire and ability in their calling, but where is the specific Biblical pointer to this? Here it is:

So Christ himself gave the apostles, the prophets, the evangelists, the pastors and teachers, to equip his people for works of service, so that the body of Christ may be built up until we all reach unity in the faith and in the knowledge of the Son of God and become mature, attaining to the whole measure of the fullness of Christ. (Ephesians 4:11-13)

Some are called for this great office and the duty of these evangelists is not just to evangelise, but to equip His people for works of service, in other words *to teach others to evangelise.* Because, after all, we are all bound by the *Great Commission*, the defining 'mission statement' of the Christian faith:

Therefore go and make disciples of all nations, baptizing them in the name of the Father and of the Son and of the Holy Spirit, and teaching them to obey everything I have commanded you. And surely I am with you always, to the very end of the age. (Matthew 28:19-20)

So yes, we must *all* yearn for spiritual gifts. And we must *all* evangelise. We must *all* attempt to reach a World gone mad. We must *all* venture into the Lion's Den.

Be alert and of sober mind. Your enemy the devil prowls around like a roaring lion looking for someone to devour. (1 Peter 5:8)

Our culture has been thoroughly infiltrated by those who wish to impose a totalitarian State *without anyone noticing.* They have chosen to use artificial 'victim groups' as their means of accomplishing this, to wrench society from traditional Christian structures and redefine the way that society functions. What this actually means is that these 'victims' are just pawns in the process and are, in fact, victims *of society,* rather than victims protected by society.

These people need to be set free and the only person who can do this is Jesus himself.

Hopefully this book may help in some way.

Appendix A: Could Cultural Marxism be a conspiracy theory?

In the Preface and elsewhere I noted that Cultural Marxism is either a real conspiracy, or that *believing in it* was the actual conspiracy. This book follows the hard evidence and takes the first view, but there are many who disagree. So we will now summarise their reasons for disagreement:

1. Unsavoury bedfellows

On the day *Anders Breivik* shot dead 69 members of a Norwegian workers youth league on the island of Utoya in July 2011, he released his 'manifesto', where he stated that Cultural Marxism was responsible for mass Muslim immigration into Europe, in order to undermine traditional European values. This is *fear by association*, when one is reminded that Cultural Marxism is given as the source of most of the Western World's problems by some on the far-right, usually dressed up as a Jewish conspiracy, due to the fact that most key initiators were from a Jewish background. This is not helped when one discovers that William Lind and Paul Weyrich, the first two commentators to extensively refer to Cultural Marxism, are both from the right-wing of conservatism, with a passionate disregard of those from the far-left. Of course this is awkward for those of us coming from a politically neutral perspective and the wisest and most honest thing we can do is to consciously divorce ourselves from any unsavoury associations and follow our own God-given conscience in our search for the truth.

2. Mainstream failures

Many detractors would remark that, if Cultural Marxism is true, why hasn't it made more inroads in front-line politics over the last few decades? They point out that, if academia has been churning out students brainwashed with far-left ideologies, how come capitalism is still going well (rather than the workers rising up to own the means of production) and that mainstream politics seems to have been unaffected too, with far more right-wing leaning governments over the last few years. My answer is that Marxism, whether 'economic' or 'cultural' is such a failure of a concept that 'knocking at the front door' is always going to get the door slammed in your face and that its only chance is through stealth and subtle promptings, dressed up as 'political correctness' or 'postmodernism' which, as the story of Part One of this book has shown, has, in fact, been remarkably successful.

3. Blame our materialistic capitalistic society

Some would say that the World we have inherited is the result of natural market forces driven by our capitalistic society, rather than attributing all the things we don't like to the machinations of an imaginary cabal of Marxist professors. It is true that most of the Frankfurt School were correct in their analysis of the evils of materialism and capitalism and how it reduces the population to one-dimensional consumers, created simply to service the system. Of course Cultural Marxism has not created this environment, but it has ridden it like a rodeo performer, working on its weaknesses to control its direction, with great patience. Capitalism is value-free, the very antithesis of altruism, so if there's a buck to be made in the 'pink economy', for instance, then *'hi ho silver', let us all ride that horse.*

4. You are being sucked into others' paranoia

A popular figure quoted here would be Andrew Breitbart, simply because of the success of the *Breitbart News Network*, (supposedly Donald Trump's favourite news source) although he himself died in 2012. In his autobiography he describes his discovery of Cultural Marxism as his 'awakening'. In the words of a detractor, Scott Oliver, this was the moment *'that all conspiracy cranks feel when the vast, anxiety-inducing complexity of the universe becomes pacified in the paranoiac, pattern-seeking mind, reduced to the imaginary order of some joined-up plot ... Grasping its effects, he said shortly before his death in 2012, was like "putting the medicine in the sherbet... My one great epiphany, my one a-ha moment where I said, 'I got it—I see what exactly happened in this country.'"*[1] Attitudes like this marked Breitbart out as an enemy of the far-left. And, of course, defamation is a key tactic of Cultural Marxists, character assassination by any other name.

5. Nazi associations

This is a sinister slant, but is a constant theme of the group of YouTube videos that I have just binge-watched – on your behalf – of those who wish to debunk the very idea of Cultural Marxism. They attempt to colour their targets with a nazi, fascist brush, on the flimsy premise that Cultural Marxism is a direct descendant of *Cultural Bolshevism*, supposedly the device used by the Nazi party to de-humanise the Jews and indoctrinate the German people into the idea that Jews were intent on taking over the World. Yes, the Nazis did have this opinion of the Jews, but they didn't call it Cultural Bolshevism, which was simply a reaction to the state of art and music at that time. When you have read Part One of this book you will recognise the tactic of the dehumanising of those one disagrees with, but the saddest thing is that the presenters of these YouTube videos are all young people who have been fed a lie and appear to lack the will or desire to check their facts.

+ + + + + + + + + + + +

My blanket response to all of the above is that we should *follow the evidence* and if you are reading this as a prelude to Part One of the book, you will find there enough hard evidence to convince every fair-minded person that our World is currently going through such a rapid change of culture that the only possible explanation for this is that we are all players in a grand design, at the mercy of whoever is 'pulling the strings'.

NOTES

[1] https://www.vice.com/en_us/article/78mnny/unwrapping-the-conspiracy-theory-that-drives-the-alt-right

Appendix B: My sources
'Controversial' sources

This book was sparked off by a viewing of a YouTube video by Jordan Peterson, recommended by a Facebook friend. Subsequently my researches took me to many places but I can honestly say that the following commentators and analysts have been the most useful for me:

Jordan Peterson is a Canadian clinical psychologist, cultural critic and professor of psychology at the University of Toronto.

Stefan Molyneux is a right wing Canadian podcaster and YouTuber with over 650,000 subscribers.

Dave Rubin is an American liberal political commentator with an online talk show, the *Rubin Report*, with over 500,000 subscribers.

Rocking Mr E is a Welsh YouTuber with 18,000 subscribers, describing himself as socially conservative and economically liberal.

Sam Harris is an American neuroscientist and philosopher with the *Waking Up* podcast, each receiving downloads in the tens of thousands.

Dennis Prager is an American conservative radio talk show host. His *PragerU* video archive has over a million subscribers.

Ben Shapiro is a hugely popular cultural commentator and is the scourge of the far-left. His YouTube vlog regularly attracts 500,000+ views. He is an orthodox Jew and proudly wears his yarmulke, even when debating with the most virulent of activists.

I can say at the outset that none of these people are traditional Christians, many are atheists, some are gay, some are Jewish, some are just left of centre, others are just right (of centre). Yet the insights given and the freedom in which they operate are so refreshing, particularly now that there are, usually, no sponsors to pacify, as most are financed directly by subscribers. There really needs to be one or two Christian voices here though it is understandable that we should be concentrating our efforts in rescuing people from the Kingdom of the World, not critiquing it. Yet one thing seems to unify them and this is significant – *apart from avowed atheist Sam Harris, they all defend the Judeo-Christian worldview and identify it as the single unifying force for a stable society.* My two favourites on the above list are David Rubin because of the quality of his guests and his laid-back style and Rocking Mr E, for his clarity and passion and the wicked guitar licks in his show ident!

Frequent guests of these people include two pantomime villains of the MSM (Mainstream Media), Nigel Farage and Katie Hopkins. Both are vilified because they don't fit the acceptable mould and often voice what others are thinking and dare not vocalise. Hopkins admitted this in a recent interview and her 800k+ twitter followers bear testimony to this fact. But the fact remains that we are programmed to consider both as pariahs and it is likely that their voices in the MSM will be gradually phased out. Yet if you listen to them being interviewed by a sympathetic listener (Dave Rubin comes to mind) you hear articulate, concerned and intelligent human beings who are not afraid to speak their mind even if it makes them unpopular with the powers that be (and those who are influenced by the powers that be).

Appendix C:
Useful resources

There are a number of useful resources that have been used obliquely in the preparation of this book. We have not over-burdened this book with 'quotes' and 'citations', except where absolutely necessary. Readers are encouraged to undertake their own further research should they want to get into some of the detail at a more granular level. We find these resources useful:

GENERAL BOOKS

Global Disorder – Robert Harvey – 2003
ISBN1-84119-832-2, *especially Chapter 13 "The New Communists?"*

Stepping Into the Shadows – Why Women Convert to Islam – Rosemary Sookhdeo – 2007

Belief and The Nation – John Scriven – 2013
Wilberforce Publications – ISBN 9780-9575725-08

Deluded, Deceived or Discipled? – Martin Panter
2008 – Actsco.Org – ISBN 978-974-16-5197-9

Christians in The Firing Line – Dr Richard Scott 2013
Wilberforce Publications – ISBN 9780-9575725-15

One Flesh – *What Jesus Teaches About Love, Relationships, Marriage and A Lot More ......* – Peter Sammons – 2012
Christian Publications International

The Empty Promise of Godism – Reflections on the Multi-Faith Agenda – Peter Sammons – 2009
Christian Publications International

The Church In Crisis – David N Samuel – 2004 –
The Association of the Continuing Church Trust

The Big Lie: *Exposing the Nazi roots of the American Left*
Dinesh D'Souza – 2017 – Ingram Publisher Services
ISBN 978-1621573487

The Strange Death of Europe – Douglas Murray 2017
Bloomsbury Continuum – ISBN 978-1472942241

The Death of Western Christianity – Patrick Sookhdeo
2017 – Isaac Publishing – ISBN 978-0997703344

Gospel Witness: *Defending and extending the Kingdom of
God* – Joseph Boot – Wilberforce Publications
ISBN 978-0995683266

PERIODICALS – SPECIFIC EDITIONS

The Economist – Social Media's Threat To Democracy
November 4th-10th 2017

The Economist – Gendercide – *What Happened to 100
Million Baby Girls?* – March 6th-12th 2010

The Spectator – *Don't Even Think It! Thought Crime
Special:* Melanie Phillips, Alan Rusbriger, Matthew
Parris, Christopher Booker – 18 September 2010

PERIODICALS – GENERAL EDITIONS

Sword – *the Unchanging Word of God* (bi-monthly, UK)
the author is a regular contributor.
http://www.swordmagazine.net

Prophecy Today – Monthly, online,
http://www.prophecytoday.uk/

Now why don't you ... ?

At the current time twenty of Steve's books are available for purchase, either through Christian bookshops or directly from www.sppublishing.com

To Life!
Rediscovering Biblical Church

Have you ever asked the question, where does the World end and the Church begin? Is the 21st Century Church truly the best it could possibly be?

How the Church lost The Way...
... and how it can find it again

The story of how the Church has been infiltrated by a pagan virus that has worked its way through every facet of our Christian life and how we can start fighting back.

How the Church lost The Truth...
... and how it can find it again

What has happened to some key battlegrounds of Christian Truth and how it is that the Church has managed to lose so much that had been revealed to it in the Bible.

Jesus, the Man of Many Names
A Fresh Understanding from the dawn of time to the End of Days

A book about Jesus that does offer fresh insights without boasting new revelations. Drawing on sources from the Jewish world, ancient and modern, the author will take you on an exhilarating, lively and entertaining exploration of the life and times of the Jewish Messiah.

The Truth is out there
The Ultimate World Conspiracy. Who really is pulling the strings?

Is history just a random sequence of events, or are there secret manipulations? What makes us tick? How did the World as we see it come to be? Read this book if you are prepared to be challenged.

The (other) F-Word
Faith, the Last Taboo

A presentation of the Gospel for the modern world. It is direct, uncompromising, engaging and is written to be relevant to the everyday person. Dare you go where modern man fears to tread? You'll either be inspired or provoked, either way it should be an interesting experience.

Outcast Nation
Israel, The Jews ... and You

The story of the People and the Land through biblical and secular history, tracing the outworkings of God's covenants and offering explanations for both the survival and the success of this Outcast Nation.

God's Signature
The Wonders of the Hebrew Scriptures

Have you ever wondered how the Old Testament came to be written, why God chose Hebrew as the language of the Book and what exactly could we be missing through not reading the Hebrew Scriptures in their original language?

The Bishop's New Clothes
Has the Church Sold out to the World?

Is the Church as it should be or has it sold out to the World? Is the Body of Christ doing all it could as God's ambassadors or is there room for not so much an improvement as a complete overhaul? This book pulls no punches, but it does so engagingly, with wit and warmth.

God's Blueprint
What does the Old Testament really say?

You will discover recurring themes that build up a wonderful picture of God, the actions and teachings of the Biblical prophets in context, the benefits of viewing the Scriptures Hebraically and new insights revealed by the One New Man Bible translation.

God's Tapestry
What do we do with the Hebrew Scriptures?

This book scratches where most of the Church is itching and cuts right to the heart of some of the controversies concerning how we should be reading and acting on God's Word today.

Hebraic Church
Thinking Differently

Hebraic Church? Now there's a phrase designed to upset or confuse just about everyone. Yet being Hebraic is not what many in the Church imagines it to be. In fact it could be nothing less than the key for true restoration and revival.

Hope

Is there any hope in the World?

Here is a book written to stir the heart of the average citizen of today's world by challenging them to think beyond the here and now. It pulls no punches as it provides a creeping crescendo of revelation regarding man and his relationship with God and how the Church has mostly failed in its mission to mirror the image of Jesus.

Livin' the Life

Christianity rediscovered

Using tools developed over the last few years, the author re-examines a wide spectrum of what we think and how we act as followers of Jesus Christ. To move forwards in our faith we really need to go back to the very beginning.

Zionion

Why does the World obsess over Israel?

What's with the British government, the Palestinians, the United Nations, the media, activists, academics, boycotters, some Jews (!), Jihadists, some Christians, neo-Nazis and conspiracy buffs?

The Easter Telling

Easter explained in a Passover service

In this small booklet you have all that you need to re-create this service, primarily following the script indicated in the Gospel accounts, but always in the context of the events of the Exodus, the backdrop of the Passover celebration.

Water
The Stuff of Life

This small book takes you on a fascinating journey into the world of water. From a brief analysis of its structure and unique properties, we look at its function in our bodies and then wonder how it gets to us, through natural means and human ingenuity. We also see its significance in world religions but also see its darker side.

Blood
The River of Life

When it comes to connections, nothing does it better than blood. Silently and unseen it performs its tasks within our body. But it doesn't stop there, blood is identified with other functions that stretch into community, heritage and even further into very surprising places.

Bread
The Food of Life

This small book explores the world of bread. From its origins and history, we look at how it has been made and see it as a metaphor of how our world has gained a degree of complexity, yet has failed in feeding everyone.